BUILD
a BETTER LIFE

PRACTICAL TOOLS AND STRATEGIES
TO DEVELOP AND LEAD
YOUR LIFE AND BUSINESS
THE WAY JESUS WOULD.

BRANDON
SCHAEFER

BUILD A BETTER LIFE
©2015 by **BRANDON SCHAEFER**

For information, write to Five Capitals, PO Box 290 Pawleys Island, SC 29585, USA or www.fivecapitals.net

First printing 2015
Printed via Createspace in the United States.

Cover & Interior Design: Pete Berg
Photos: Julie Marshall

ISBN: 978-0-9966858-0-1

DEDICATION

This book is dedicated to all Christians who are serious about going after a healthy, productive, integrated and fulfilling life.

The thief comes only to steal and kill and destroy;
I have come that they may have life, and have it to the full.
— John 10:10

Acknowledgements

As the famous quote from Sir Isaac Newton states: "We all stand on the shoulders of giants." This reality is certainly the case for this book. I'm grateful for the many mentors, teachers and guides who have invested in me over the years. These pages are the combination of the many conversations, books, lectures, seminars, workshops and coaching calls of which I've had the privilege to be a part.

Specifically, I would like to thank:

Mike Breen's continual investment over four steady years was invaluable. Many of the foundational teachings found in this book are his.

Dave Rhodes provided key material as well—serving as a constant friend and sounding board—as he worked with me to craft the message and content to ensure it both stirs and sticks.

Ben Sternke was great to collaborate around (as well as improving and innovating) some of the Five Capitals material found in *Oikonomics*, his co-authored book (with Mike Breen).

Mikaela Schaefer worked tirelessly with me to see the book to completion, offering writing, editing and creative insights and serving as project manager to see the pages get to print.

A special thanks to Matt Tebbe, Judy Keene, Robert Neely, Pete Berg, the Five Capitals leadership team, Frontier leaders and coaching participants for their invaluable reflections, testimonies and insights.

Thanks to my good friend Charles, who otherwise wishes to remain anonymous, yet provided the financial fuel to get the book to print. We are grateful.

Lastly, thanks to my lovely wife T.J.—for her constant encouragement, belief in the project, sacrifice, love and support.

Thank you all,

Brandon

TABLE OF CONTENTS

INTRODUCTION:
JESUS ISN'T WHAT HE SEEMS ... AGAIN

It is not the beauty of a building you should look at;
it's the construction of the foundation that will stand the test of time.
— David Allan Coe[1]

By the grace God has given me, I laid a foundation as a wise builder, and someone else is building on it. But each one should build with care. For no one can lay any foundation other than the one already laid, which is Jesus Christ.
— 1 Corinthians 3:10-11

WWJDIHWM?

Have you noticed how the 1970s won't stay in the past? A few years back, boot cut jeans were in vogue, along with paisley shirts and flowered skirts. My guess is that, if I looked in your jeans drawer, you would probably still have a pair or two. Still, what are boot cut jeans, but a modern version of bell-bottoms? Hippies of the 1970s unite! We've even made parodies of this nostalgia with programs like *That '70s Show* and the ongoing, never-ending reruns and new episodes of *Scooby-Doo*. (How many reboots can one cartoon have?)

All to say, if you watch culture closely enough, and long enough, you'll find that most "new" styles are not new at all. Culture, along with all its artifacts (fashion, art, language), tends to be cyclical.

Trends in the Christian subculture have a similar life cycle. No doubt you remember the WWJD craze of the early 1990s. A youth pastor in Michigan started wearing a bracelet with the letters that stood for *What Would Jesus Do?* as a way to help her students remain conscious of Jesus' moral and ethical example. Seemingly overnight Christians everywhere donned such bracelets to help them remember that compelling question.

Of course, this trend wasn't new either. "What Would Jesus Do?" was the subtitle of Charles Sheldon's 1896 book, *In His Steps*. A century later the only new thing was putting this phrase on a rubber bracelet.

We don't need to bring the phrase WWJD back just yet. It took almost 100 years for its first comeback. We don't want to rush culture, after all. But this question remains a salient one for marketplace Christians—if we make one small addition:

*What Would Jesus Do **If He Were Me?***

What would Jesus do if he were living in my circumstances with my skills, gifts and interests? What would he do if he had my spouse? My boss? My 1993 Nissan Maxima that needs a new transmission?

Dallas Willard said, "Disciples of Jesus are those who are with him, learning to be like him. That is, they are learning to lead their life—their actual existence—as he would lead their life if he were they."

Would Jesus have another child?[2]

Would he go for the promotion?

Would he sell the car for scrap and bike to work?

WHAT WOULD JESUS DO IF HE WERE ME?

Would he go for the next level in Candy Crush, watch just one more episode on Netflix before bed, or spring for the exterior wax and wheel shine?

This isn't just a rubber-bracelet question. It's actually the only way to understand Paul's charge in 1 Corinthians 11:1, which says to "imitate me, as I imitate Christ." Paul didn't *literally* do everything

Jesus did. Instead, he made tents and traveled the Greco-Roman world as *Jesus would have done had Jesus been Paul.*

WHAT DO I HAVE IN COMMON WITH A CELIBATE JEWISH MAN WHO LIVED 2,000 YEARS AGO?

To imitate Jesus is to become the kind of person who lives my life as Jesus would if he were me. If Christianity is to have a significant force in our world, if it is to be meaningful and practical for Christians who name themselves after Jesus, we must ask ourselves: "What would Jesus look like if he lived in my skin? What would he be like in my life and my situation, at work, play, and home?"

Recently, my wife and I hosted extended family at our house. I took the opportunity to run this idea past an older, godly relative of mine. I was struck by her response. "Oh! That's impossible! I could never live my life as though Jesus were me! He was God, after all!" That's true—of course Jesus was fully God. But he was also fully human.

So what kind of human being was Jesus, and how relevant are the things he did to my day-to-day life?

What do I have in common with a celibate Jewish man who lived 2,000 years ago?

Thankfully, we get some answers in Mark 6.

> Jesus left there and went to his hometown, accompanied by his disciples. When the Sabbath came, he began to teach in the synagogue, and many who heard him were amazed. "Where did this man get these things?" they asked. "What's this wisdom that has been given him, that he even does miracles! Isn't this the carpenter? Isn't this Mary's son and the brother of James, Joseph, Judas and Simon? Aren't his sisters here with us?" And they took offense at him. Jesus said to them, "Only in his hometown, among his relatives and in his own house is a prophet without honor." He could not do

any miracles there, except lay his hands on a few sick people and heal them. And he was amazed at their lack of faith. Then Jesus went around teaching from village to village. — Mark 6:1-6

Jesus' hometown and even his own family doubted that this kid from their town could be the Messiah prophesied in the Old Testament. Not only did they doubt him—they tried to kill him.[3] If Jesus' hometown had a "You are now entering Nazareth, Population 450" sign beside the road, you can be sure that "Home of Jesus Christ, the one who takes away the sins of the world" was not printed on it.

In these people's minds, Jesus couldn't have been a prophet or a teacher because he was (just) a carpenter. In Mark 6, the Greek word for carpenter is *tekton*. Tekton means artisan or craftsman or builder—someone who made things with their hands. But when *tekton* occurs in our English Bibles, it's usually translated as carpenter.

The first translations of the Latin Bible into English were personally translated by John Wycliffe, who desired to put the Bible into the hands of common people. In 14th century Western Europe, wood was plentiful, and so it was the primary material used for building. Wycliffe contextualized the word *tekton* for his audience by using the familiar and accessible translation *carpenter*. Unfortunately, in our modern day, because we have so many specializations for building such as contractors, electricians, engineers and architects, we think Jesus was merely a carpenter who built chairs and tables.[4]

> SO IT'S SAFE TO SAY JESUS WASN'T MERELY JUST A CARPENTER, HE WAS AND IS JESUS THE BUILDER.

In first century, Palestinian people rarely built things with wood. The primary building material was stone. It is more likely that Jesus was a stonemason than a woodworking carpenter. So it's safe to say Jesus wasn't merely just a carpenter, he was and is **Jesus the Builder**. (Some of you may need to peel off a bumper sticker after hearing that.) From what we know about Jesus' earthly father Joseph, we know that Jesus came from a long line of builders, going all the way back to David. Today artisans and builders are trained to be specialists, but in first-century Palestine, people had to be both generalists and specialists. They were the general contractors, the architects and the on-site team leaders. They did it all from beginning to end.

So we can say with great confidence that Jesus was a part of a family business of master builders. Jesus, it seems, was a small business owner—and a successful one at that. Why else would he use so much business language and metaphor in his teaching? He spoke about investment, taxes, return on investment, and the economies of his day. In a climactic moment, he returned to the images he was most familiar with by telling Peter, "On this rock I will build my church."[5] Jesus named his right-hand man—the one he knew and worked with the best—Peter (i.e. Rocky). In addition, Jesus concluded his masterful Sermon on the Mount with the parable of the wise and foolish builders, teaching that one who builds on the rock has the humility to hear and the courage to obey Jesus' word.[6]

Assuming Jesus was 30 when he began his public ministry with his baptism in the river Jordan, it's safe to conclude he was a business leader for close to 15 years. He was a businessman at heart. So as we try to discover what Jesus would do if he were us, we need to look through the lens of business.

As business leaders we must wrestle with the fact that Jesus was the smartest businessman who ever lived and that he built the most successful business the world has ever seen. We're not talking about his stone masonry (though it probably looked incredible) but about the business of building his church. Consider this: the business Jesus built is over 2,000 years old and has three billion followers in the present day alone. It is staffed by many employees who volunteer their time and finance the enterprise. People have freely given their lives rather than quit this business. Jesus wasn't just a great teacher, but also a great businessman and leader. It's safe to say that he can teach us how to build a life worth living for.

So let's get to know Jesus the Builder.

Discussion Questions

1. What trends have you noticed cycling through our Christian culture?

2. What would Jesus do if he were living in your circumstances with your skills, gifts and interests?

3. Do you need to reframe your perspective of Jesus as a builder? As a business professional? And as a leader?

4. What has Jesus already built in and around your life?

5. In your working life, where are the opportunities to make Jesus more relevant? To let him into your life?

Putting It Into Practice

Jay Hidalgo, Marketing, Sales, and Business Coach

It's so simple, yet so profound. Jesus is the best (*insert any occupation here*) who ever lived. And yet, for most of my working life, I limited him by only inviting him into my business dealings when "major" issues came up. Through the practical concepts in this book, I've come to learn that Jesus gives insight on finance, marketing, sales, human resources, "work-life" balance, non-profit organizations, planning and anything else you can think of. I encourage everyone to dive into these pages and apply these principles to your life, and see for yourself how Jesus' teachings will equip you to have a full, integrated life. Then ask yourself one simple question: *Do I believe him or not?*

CHAPTER ONE
PERSPECTIVE:
JESUS THE BUILDER

A little perspective, like a little humor, goes a long way.
— Allen Klein

I am the way and the truth and the life.
No one comes to the Father except through me.
— John 14:6

Jesus the Builder of Better Stories

It was my sophomore year at Iowa State University, and life could not have been going better. I had just completed a great summer internship with Motorola in Austin, Texas, learning a lot, creating new friendships and enjoying Austin, where I soaked up the live music, tubed down the Guadalupe River and ate at numerous fantastic restaurants. Before returning to Iowa State, I had secured my next summer internship with Motorola at their European headquarters in Glasgow, Scotland. My freshmen year at Iowa State had gone well, too. I was freshman class president of my fraternity (Alpha Gamma Rho), elected freshman council president of the university and found myself enjoying many of the Greek community's social activities, not to mention the freedom of being on my own.

I can confidently say that I was sure of myself and knew where I wanted to go.

So that September, while politely saying hello to my new freshman fraternity brothers, I found my way to Adam's room. When I walked in, I immediately noticed the Bible on his desk.

I grew up going to church every week, but for me it was more of a social engagement. I looked forward to seeing my friends and going out to eat afterward. I'd gone through confirmation and had adopted the perspective that if I did good, God would bless me—an attitude that had followed me to Iowa State. Although I didn't attend every week (it was pretty boring), I had found a small church close to campus that had a late-morning service. (Given how Saturday nights usually went, I wasn't going before 11 a.m.)

I said to Adam, "So you go to church? I do too." I told him about the church I went to just down the street and said he'd be welcome to join me.

"Well I already have a church I've been going to for a few weeks," he said. "My sister is a junior here, so I've been going to the church she's involved in."

"Gotcha," I replied.

"Tell you what—if you like your church we can go there this weekend, and then try my church the following weekend," he offered.

It sounded like a fair enough plan to me. I wasn't married to my church, and who knows—his might be better. After all, his church had an 11 a.m. service, too. The visit to my church went as I'd expected—boring. Neither of us said much afterward; it was what it was. The next Saturday Adam found me and said his sister would pick us up around 10:30 the next morning so we could check out his church. I was blown away from the very beginning. There were tons of cars, and it took us 10 minutes just to park. Everyone was very friendly, and they had their own café area complete with free coffee and donuts. Already I had lost my bearings.

"What kind of church is this?" I asked, obviously referring to the Starbucks in the middle of the church. Adam and Nicole didn't seemed to be too phased by it and said that the church was going for a more welcoming and modern feel. We walked through more doors into the back of what seemed like a very new auditorium complete with stadium seating and an enormous stage.

Five minutes later the rock band started. I didn't ask where the organ was or when we were going to sing "Be Thou My Vision" because I knew they didn't have one and that song wasn't on their list. Long story short, my idea of church was shot to pieces in 56 minutes. I loved every minute of it—the buzz, the energy of the young people, great music and the relevant message. Although the atmosphere and experience highly impressed me, I was most impacted by the biblically based message. It spoke to me and my situation—and could be applied to my selfish, all-consuming college life.

FOR THE FIRST TIME I WAS INTERESTED IN WHAT THE BIBLE HAD TO SAY AND HOW GOD COULD BE *REAL* AND *RELEVANT* TO MY LIFE.

By now you probably get where this is going. Adam and some great leaders from both the church and Campus Crusade began to invest in and disciple me. For the first time I was interested in what the Bible had to say and how God could be *real* and *relevant* to my life. I made a decision to follow Christ—with all my heart, soul and strength—before the winter break.

Without skipping a beat the trajectory of my life changed, as God started writing a better story. Change was all around me—change for the better, and change with my best in mind. God was building in me, through me and around me. *He was building a better life for me.*

Accepting that too much of my life was "all about me," I began to question:

Do I need to swear so much?

Is all this pizza and beer good for me?

And on a larger scale, What do I really want to do with my life?

As I started to press into what God wanted, I sensed him leading me to study abroad. Ironically, no one really supported this decision (in an agricultural fraternity, no one studies in Spain), but it didn't matter because now I was listening to a new voice. This voice eventually moved me to change majors, because—who was I kidding—I wasn't into farming that much anyway. Yes, I grew up on a farm, and even today the skills and work ethic my dad instilled in me still prove invaluable. It just wasn't my passion.

Allowing God to speak into the next steps of my life has taken time, with steps forward and steps back. But through my college years God changed the way I looked at Jesus and the power of what he did on the cross, not only to save us from our sin, but also to save us from our broken stories.

In that pivotal point of my sophomore year, I learned firsthand how Jesus came to recreate and redeem our lives here. Whether we are at home or at work, Jesus wants to help us write a bigger, better story—one that has more fulfillment, integration and lasting significance than we can even imagine.

Through the years, working in both the corporate and ministry sectors, I have encountered lots of individuals in all walks of life who are searching for a better story. What is true of the entirety of our western culture is true everywhere—even in the business world, where people are crying out to be a part of something larger than themselves.

Marketing Inadequacy or Empowerment?

If you look close enough, you can see businesses working hard to draw people into a bigger story by making the shift from inadequacy marketing—*buy this car and people will love you*—to empowerment marketing—*buy this car and fully realize your potential.* We see this with messages such as Nike's *Just Do It,* Lowes' *Let's build something together* and Home Depot's *You can build it. We can help.*

Unfortunately, marketers often understand, better than many Christians, that the stories we live are powerful. Inadequacy marketing seeks to capitalize on a sense of lack, highlighting and magnifying how awful the lack is and then offering a solution (i.e. a product) that will fix our lack. Advertisers use inadequacy marketing primarily because it motivates people to make decisions based on fear, guilt and shame.

For much of the 20th century, this was the dominant way marketing and advertising functioned, and the inadequacy story had such a powerful impact on our culture that it even showed up in our churches. In many cases, the Gospel of Jesus Christ was proclaimed using the same methodology and logic that motivated many to make decisions for Christ based on the inadequacy marketing of the Good News.

It went something like this:
"Pray the sinner's prayer, and Jesus will save you from hell."
(That's not very uplifting or empowering.)

> Lack = sin that leads to damnation
> Product = salvation
> Purchase = prayer

Now there are certainly truths in that pitch, but the question isn't whether this is true. The question is *whether this story does justice to what the Good News wants to do in us.*

For me, growing up, this was the message I internalized. Sure, it probably scared me out of doing some bad things, but it didn't encourage or inspire me to have a closer, more connected relationship with God.

The problem with a Gospel motivated by inadequacy marketing is that too many people stay there and never really shake the feeling of lack that is driven by their personal fear, guilt and/or shame. They have purchased a product that will save them from hell, but they don't expect it to change their day-to-day lives.

Jesus the Builder wants to change our daily lives.
He wants us to live better stories than his. He understands our stories are wildly powerful and meant for incredible abundance and purpose. Jesus the Builder wants to empower us to live a great, compelling story.

JESUS THE BUILDER WANTS TO CHANGE OUR DAILY LIVES.

What does Jesus proclaim coming out of the desert in Luke 4?

"The Spirit of the Lord is upon me,

for he has anointed me to bring Good News to the poor.

He has sent me to proclaim that captives will be released,

that the blind will see,

that the oppressed will be set free,

and that the time of the Lord's favor has come.

Captive people released? Sight for the blind? Oppressed set free? Favor? *Sounds pretty uplifting to me.*

Let's put this in a marketplace context. If you're a business leader, think about the employees you lead and the people you supervise. Do you want them to do their jobs because they fear getting fired? Do you want your workers to perform their responsibilities out of guilt or constant obligation? Do you want them to sit back in shame, lacking confidence to ever pitch a new idea? And is that how you want to be led by *your* boss or board?

Of course not! You want to be the boss who motivates with empowerment, courage and inspiration—and incidentally your employees want that, too.

Thankfully Jesus the Builder told a better story than one of inadequacy. His good news is about empowering in spite of and in the midst of our shortcomings. Ultimately, inadequacy is not the leverage used to motivate; it's the backdrop on which we are *empowered* in forgiveness and freedom.

An inadequacy gospel tends to produce people who take care of their lack, avoid the (eternal) consequences of their sin and hunker down to survive their compartmentalized lives. This is not the life Jesus desires for us. He wants our story to be compelling and contagious. He wants us to live with God at the center of our story, at home, work and in our communities.

When we give Jesus who we are and what we are called to do, he is able to build something to his glory. This is the guy who said, "I have come so you may have life to the full!"[7] He didn't come to give us forgiveness and just enough strength for us to hang on for retirement and shuffleboard; he came to give us real, lasting, meaningful, significant life. This is the life Jesus offers—empowered by his grace and truth, so that we may thrive in every area of life.

The Builder's Materials: *Words, Works, and Ways*

After becoming a Christian in college, I seriously studied the Bible for the first time, desiring to know what exactly it says and how it could be applied to my life. However, I only took Jesus at his *word* for my personal life. I never really thought about looking at Jesus' word for my working life. I unwittingly created a paradigm in which I separated the secular from the sacred. Jesus—who *is the Word* and is revealed *through the Word*—spoke to me personally as Brandon, the Christian, but I didn't listen for his word as Brandon, the businessman. I lived a segmented, compartmentalized life. Sure, I knew God was the Creator of the world—so maybe he could have some insight into my work—but generally I wasn't there yet.

This understanding did not take place until I lived in Scotland, and friends started to challenge me about the *works* of Jesus. I attended a great evangelical church (Westwood Hill in East Kilbride, just outside of Glasgow) that challenged me to be the same person at work that I was at home. As a result, I made an effort to focus on the ethics and practices of Jesus at work. This was the first time I began to ask WWJDIHWM? at work. This was truly life-changing. I now began to think about the *word* and *works* of Jesus together. But I still didn't really think Jesus had anything to say about the way I approached the work, especially from a strategic and profitability standpoint. For the best "ways to work," I relied on the *Harvard Business Review*, books like *Good to Great* and other business resources. They were the authority on work.

It was easy to imagine how Jesus built his artisan business. He used the same raw materials (stone, mortar) as others, but after the age of 30 or so, Jesus began to build something else. He began to build into other people—his disciples—and to announce the coming Kingdom of God. He called this "building" the church.

In short, I saw that in order to fully engage with Jesus as a businessman, I needed to look at three essential components of Jesus' life and business: *his word, his works and his way.*[8]

Since this revelation I've seen the power of integrating the way of Jesus in my work life as well. By the *way* I'm referring to Jesus' strategic methods and means. For Jesus, the means didn't justify the ends—the means were the ends. He didn't ask if his methods were effective. He looked for faithful methods that would bear fruit. His goal was never just to get things done or to gain a platform or to win approval. The way of Jesus is not simply utility; rather it is the texture that envelops his *word* and *works*. Jesus maps out ways for us to do our work as business leaders and professionals so we can have integration, fulfillment and impact in every area of our lives.

> Jesus answered, "I am the way and the truth and the life. No one comes to the Father except through me." — John 14:6

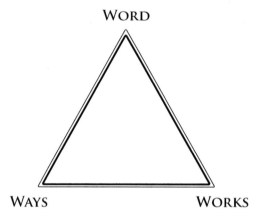

Most people do not want to take their work home with them. But what would it look like to be serious enough about following Jesus that we take our home to work, both in terms of our ethics and principles and in the methods and ways we go about our work?

> ## BUT WHAT WOULD IT LOOK LIKE TO BE SERIOUS ENOUGH ABOUT FOLLOWING JESUS THAT WE TAKE OUR HOME TO WORK.

The aim of this book is not only to build you up and encourage you, but to invite you to join us as we seek how Jesus wants to build his words, his works and his ways into each of us. We want to help you build your professional life in such a way that it impacts the kingdom of God, and to build something of lasting significance so you can write a story better than you could even imagine.

All wisdom comes from God, so rather than making secular sources our go-to source for business wisdom, we will look at what the Bible says about how to run a business based on what we see in Jesus the Builder and his disciples, starting with Peter.

Peter: A Case Study

Looking at Peter's life we see he was a businessman just like us, most likely part of a successful family enterprise, as we know he owned his own boat. Like most of us, Peter worked hard to build his business and provide for his family.

"Peter, then known as Simon, was a Jewish leader and was working as a businessman when he met Jesus. Andrew, Peter's brother, had been so excited after hearing John the Baptist speak that he ran to tell Peter, exclaiming, "We have found the Messiah." So Andrew brought Simon to Jesus, and Jesus looked at Simon and said, "You are Simon son of John. You will be called Cephas" (translated Peter).[9]

▶ ENROLLED ▶

It's quite the introduction. I imagine Peter was thinking, "Andrew, could you tell him I already have a name? It's Simon. Why would I want to have a name that means rock—like those dang pebbles that get in our sandals every day?"

However, if we look deeper into the text, we see two things are revealed as Peter encounters Jesus for the first time. First, we see a *longing*. The backstory is that the Jewish people were desperate for a savior. Isn't that true of people today as well? Whether people realize it, they fill their hearts with things that aren't lasting—more stuff, status or prestige.

Andrew believed Jesus would finally quench that thirst, and perhaps he also

> **HIS LIFE WAS NO LONGER ABOUT BUILDING SOMETHING FOR HIMSELF; IT WAS NOW ABOUT TAKING PART IN WHAT JESUS WAS BUILDING— EVEN IF HE WASN'T COMPLETELY AWARE OF IT YET.**

would finally rid Israel of the oppression of Roman rule. Peter would, of course, be excited by this. He was striving away, trying to keep the business going and provide for his family. He had the same longing as his brother, but no way to fulfill it—until Jesus came along.

Second, we see an *enrollment* of Peter. We see the *possibility of change* and a *vision of the future* in the new name Jesus gave Peter.

This is also true of us. We don't really understand what lies ahead, yet while everything isn't clear, there is excitement in this enrollment. Peter saw that he had a possibility to build something with Jesus because he was now enrolled to follow him. His life was no longer about building something for himself; it was now about taking part in what Jesus was building—even if he wasn't completely aware of it yet.

But it doesn't stop there ...

ENROLLED ▶ EQUIPPED ▶ ENGAGED ▶ EMPTIED ▶ EMBRACED AND EMPOWERED

As Jesus continued his ministry, he knew he didn't simply need followers, but co-laborers—people to help build. It was important for Jesus to *equip* and *empower* others to carry on the work after he was gone. He needed to find out not only who was willing to follow, but also who was willing to get their hands dirty with some sacrifice, effort and surrender. Jesus tested Peter's heart by asking him to invest in the mission.

Have you ever had a hard season where God asked you to sell the car, volunteer your time at a food bank or take on a leadership role at your church? To trust him that the prize would be worth the price?

It's a test in which God is really asking, "Where is your heart? Will you trust me with this area of your life?" Have you experienced this as you've enrolled with Jesus? Have you encountered deeper levels of testing as you continue to follow him?

▶ ENROLLED ▶ EQUIPPED

It's a process with which we all must engage. In Luke we witness Peter's enrollment, the testing of his heart, and his life transformation as he responded to Jesus. Consider this passage:

> One day as Jesus stood by the Lake of Gennesaret, with the people crowding around him and listening to the word of God, he saw at the water's edge two boats, left there by the fishermen, who were washing their nets. He got into one of the boats, the one belonging to Simon, and asked him to put out a little from shore. Then he sat down and taught the people from the boat. When he had finished speaking, he said to Simon, "Put out into deep water, and let down the nets for a catch." Simon answered, "Master, we've worked hard all night and haven't caught anything. But because you say so, I will let down the nets." When they had done so, they caught such a large number of fish that their nets began to break. So they signaled their partners in the other boat to come and help them, and they came and filled both boats so full that they began to sink. When Simon Peter saw this, he fell at Jesus' knees and said, "Go away from me, Lord; I am a sinful man!" For he and all his companions were astonished at the catch of fish they had taken, and so were James and John, the sons of Zebedee, Simon's partners. Then Jesus said to Simon, "Don't be afraid; from now on you will catch men." So they pulled their boats up on shore, left everything and followed him.
> — Luke 5:1-11

There is comedy and satire in this text. We can almost hear Peter's dismissive attitude toward Jesus—Jesus, you are a builder, not a fisherman! You work with stones, not boats and nets. You don't know what you're talking about. I've fished

> # JESUS IS THE BEST ECONOMIST, LAWYER, ACTOR, TEACHER, MUSICIAN, CEO, AND MORE, AS WELL AS THE SMARTEST BUSINESSMAN THERE IS AND WILL EVER BE.

all night without catching anything. *But if you say so*, we'll go out and throw our nets on the other side. And immediately his boat was full of fish. Peter found out that Jesus is not only a great builder, but also the best fisherman the world had ever seen. Peter would learn (like we do) that Jesus is the best economist, lawyer, actor, teacher, musician, CEO and more, as well as the smartest businessman there is and will ever be. After this event, Peter got it, and he left everything to follow Jesus.

Jesus had to teach his disciples early on that he is the way for every area of life. We must learn this as well. Jesus tells us, I'll speak truth. I'll give you wisdom and insight. If you will just have the humility to hear and the courage to obey, you'll be building on solid rock. You'll be a wise builder. You will build things that really last. It can't be your way; it must be my way, because I am the greatest builder the world has ever seen.

The disciples were amazed. Not only did they see that engaging with Jesus would break them of all their perspectives and presuppositions (just as their nets almost broke), but they also saw that Jesus neither ridiculed them nor shamed them in front of the crowd gathered there. Instead, he called them with greater clarity to his vision. He did not ask them to discard what they already knew and go back to seminary, but instead conveyed the message, "I will use all your fishing skills to do something greater. I will make you fishers of men."

Peter stood amazed. He dropped everything when Jesus told him he would use all of Peter's skills and abilities to build something greater. Jesus was empowering him to greatness—to a story better than his current one. Jesus doesn't discard our past. He uses it and redeems it for even greater things.

Jesus' vision for Peter was far beyond simply striving and toiling for provision. He was moving him and the other disciples to a whole new level, not only calling them higher, but now *equipping* and *engaging* with them.

▶ EQUIPPED ▶ ENGAGED

Later on we again see Jesus speaking to the disciples' hearts by asking them, "Who do you say that I am?" or rather, as we might state it, "Who am I to you?" He was calling his disciples into an even deeper and more significant relationship—a covenant relationship, characterized by oneness with him.

> When Jesus came to the region of Caesarea Philippi, he asked his disciples, "Who do people say the Son of Man is?" They replied, "Some say John the Baptist; others say Elijah; and still others, Jeremiah or one of the prophets." "But what about you?" he asked. "Who do you say I am?" Simon Peter answered, "You are the Christ, the Son of the living God." Jesus replied, "Blessed are you, Simon son of Jonah, for this was not revealed to you by man, but by my Father in heaven. And I tell you that you are Peter, and on this rock I will build my church, and the gates of Hades will not overcome it. I will give you the keys of the kingdom of heaven; whatever you bind on earth will be bound in heaven, and whatever you loose on earth will be loosed in heaven." Then he warned his disciples not to tell anyone that he was the Christ. — Matthew 16:13-20

Jesus wanted them to understand they were now a part of his family *engaged* in the family business, no longer just fishing but building—building the kingdom of God, building into people, bringing good to earth. It's here where we finally discover the fulfillment of that mysterious name change when Jesus first met Peter. On the rock of Jesus, Peter would build his family business.

Jesus promised to use all of Peter's fishing expertise and experience to build something significant. He encouraged Peter to realize his identity here on earth and called him to build on and continue to expand the family business, even though that would involve suffering and sacrifice.

Peter was so caught up in the excitement of this new covenant relationship that, when his new covenant partner said he would have to die, Peter contradicted him. He didn't learn from the fishing incident that Jesus knows all things. Jesus quickly rebuked Peter's contradiction, saying, "Stand behind me, Satan."[10]

Peter had come a long way. He had moved from focusing on himself and his life to focusing on Jesus and partnering with him. But Peter still had further to go on this journey—recognizing that he must become less and Jesus must become greater.

For Peter, engaging fully in his new family involved one more step. Some *emptying* needed to happen in Peter to get rid of that last bit of "me." In John 18 we see the only recorded time that Peter fell away from this commitment after this enrollment into the family.

▶ ENGAGED ▶ EMPTIED

He stood just outside the courts as Jesus was being tried, and for the first time in the New Testament, a charcoal fire is mentioned as Peter three times denied knowing Jesus before the rooster's fateful crow. Peter must have been devastated. He had been so certain, when Jesus said he'd deny him, that he would not. But Jesus was right again. Peter had betrayed his covenant partner, his fellow family member in the kingdom business of building.

Then just two chapters later, in John 21, Peter went fishing again. The text specifically says that Peter declared, "I'm going fishing." He was going back to what he knew and who he was before he met Jesus—probably figuring all had been lost, given his denial and Jesus' death on the cross. Interestingly enough, the other disciples followed—likely feeling equally directionless and dejected.

Maybe you, too, have been tempted to go back on your commitment—telling yourself you've screwed up too many times or it's too hard, too tough to move forward. So you decide to return to running your business the way you used to, doing things the original way—the way things seemed to work before. You want to go back to acting as your previous self, back to when it felt like you were getting things done and providing for your family. That's what we see here: Peter emptied—emptied of his sense of "rightness" and maybe dealing with a sense of guilt over his denial, as he wondered how, given the absence of Jesus, he should proceed.

So, without skipping a beat, we once again find Peter and the disciples fishing, and of course they're catching nothing. Sound familiar? Yet there's a man on the shore telling them to cast their nets on the other side, and behold so many fish! As Peter approached the shore, he found Jesus there, cooking fish on some burning coals. Once again Peter found himself around a charcoal fire, except this time it is his teacher, Jesus, who is next to him, rather than the person Peter had denied knowing:

> "I'm going out to fish," Simon Peter told them, and they said, "We'll go with you." So they went out and got into the boat, but that night they caught nothing. Early in the morning, Jesus stood on the shore, but the disciples did not realize that it was Jesus. He called out to them, "Friends, haven't you any fish?" "No," they answered. He said, "Throw your net on the right side of the boat and you will find some." When they did, they were unable to haul the net in because of the large number of fish. Then the disciple whom Jesus loved said to Peter, "It is the Lord!" As soon as Simon Peter heard him say, "It is the Lord," he wrapped his outer garment around him (for he had taken it off) and jumped into the water. The other disciples followed in the boat, towing the net full of fish, for they were not far from shore, about a hundred yards. When they landed, they saw a fire of burning coals there with fish on it, and some bread. Jesus said to them, "Bring some of the fish you have just caught." Simon Peter climbed aboard and dragged the net ashore. It was full of large fish, 153, but even with so many the net was not torn. — John 21:3-11

Peter is reconciled and commissioned back into the family of building.

Peter journeyed from "me" to "me and Jesus" to "Jesus and me." It seems that after this embrace, Jesus was in Peter's skin. Now it's just "Jesus" for Peter.

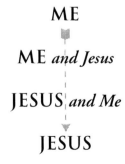

ME

ME *and Jesus*

JESUS *and Me*

JESUS

We read some of Peter's miracles and could easily picture Jesus doing them. What would Jesus be like if he were Peter? We see the answer to that in Acts, although getting there took courage and humility and some brokenness.

Peter *embraces* Jesus' ways, and as we look at his letters (1 and 2 Peter) we see that he never went back to fishing; in fact, in both of his letters, Peter used Builder language as he talked about building into the body of Christ. Take this example:

▶ EMPTIED ▶ EMBRACED & EMPOWERED

> "See, I lay a stone in Zion, a chosen and precious cornerstone, and the one who trusts in him will never be put to shame." Now to you who believe, this stone is precious. But to those who do not believe, "The stone the builders rejected has become the capstone, " and, "A stone that causes men to stumble and a rock that makes them fall." They stumble because they disobey the message—which is also what they were destined for. But you are a chosen people, a royal priesthood, a holy nation, a people belonging to God, that you may declare the praises of him who called you out of darkness into his wonderful light. — 1 Peter 2:4-9

This is the fruit of the change and transformation in the life of Peter, who was a workplace Christian just like you and me. Over the journey of his life he chose the better way, though it was sometimes the harder way, to allow Jesus' *words, works* and *ways* to envelop every area of his life. In doing so, Peter (and others) built into a line of kingdom family builders that is still under construction today. Not only that, but he also allowed himself to be *empowered* by Jesus as he *engaged* with him, and as he finally *embraced* him in all aspects of his life.

Jesus' words, works and ways became Peter's. This oneness ignited his life to be so great, in fact, that people are still building on it to this day.

If we long to have every area of our lives fully integrated and fully thriving, we must follow this same flow. That's how we will build a life worth living for and a story that's bigger than ourselves!

Peter's journey has certainly been a helpful framework in my life. Like Peter I've experienced setbacks, failing, disappointments and predictions/hopes for the future that, in retrospect, were more my plans than God's. Yet as God continued to work in Peter, so he continues to work in us. As we close out this chapter, it might be helpful to ask: *Where am I at on the journey? Enrolled? Equipped? Engaged? Being Emptied? Experiencing his Embrace? Am I stuck? Moving forward? Going backward?*

ENROLLED ▶ EQUIPPED ▶ ENGAGED ▶ EMPTIED ▶ EMBRACED AND EMPOWERED

Many people confide in me, saying, "I see the outcomes in Peter's life, but what exactly is God desiring to build in me?" While the specifics are different for everyone, I consistently see three categories of God's building process.

He desires to Build Up — To build our faith and belief in him. Jesus wants us to grow in a deeper more intimate relationship with him—growing our confidence and competence in hearing his voice so we can all the more courageously obey him. It's about trust.

He desires to Build In — To build into the community of believers that is the Body of Christ. Together we are the Church—here to be his ambassadors, to equip and encourage one another, to live together in peace and harmony and to work and move as one. We are here to challenge, correct and spur one another on. It's about being one.

He desires to Build Out — To build into our hearts a passion for the last, lost and least of this world. He wants us to live with and live out compassion, not condemnation, helping and loving our neighbors as we speak truth in love through both our words and actions, being light and life in the midst of the darkness and difficulties in this world. It's about love.

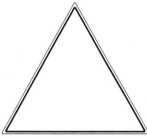

BUILD UP
(WORD TO EMPOWER YOU)

BUILD OUT
(WAYS TO EMBRACE AND EMPOWER OTHERS)

BUILD IN
(WORKS TO ENGAGE & EMPTY YOU)

Most people are either aware of, or good at, allowing God to work in one or two of these areas. Where are you today, and where is God calling you to grow?

Discussion Questions

1. What would it look like to follow Jesus in your work—both in terms of your ethics and principles and in the methods and ways you go about your work?

2. Do you feel like you lead from a place motivated by fear, guilt or shame? What can you do to motivate your co-workers, employees and family so they feel empowered to be the best they can be? What can you do to lead more with vision rather than need?

3. Have you ever had a hard season where God asked you to sell the car, give away more money or make a sacrifice for his kingdom? Was there an emptying that took place within your heart and mind? Did you see any long-term fruit from this sacrifice?

4. Is there an area of your life where God is asking you to engage with him on another level?

5. Which category—build up, build in or build out is an area of strength for you? Which needs to be an area of growth?

Putting It Into Practice

Christopher Hartenstein, President & CEO, Hartco, Inc.

In reading this chapter I was reminded that all of life is sacred and has purpose when I choose to allow my work life to conform and be directed by God. As I engage in his kingdom work through my business, lives are changed and significance in my work life is assured. I cannot think of a better way to invest my time and talents.

I own a third-generation manufacturing company in Cincinnati, OH. The business is very much a part of my calling. While I'm not overly passionate about the "widgets" we make, I do love the business relationships, as well as the family culture we've created. During certain market conditions the business has had its ups and downs. Yet as God has guided me, we've weathered the storms. How do we give God the glory? And allow him to guide every area of the business?

A great example of this is in the profits our business generates. We can and do certainly give bonuses, work to offer quality benefits to our employees and donate to charitable organizations, which are all good things. But what we have been led to do is look at our business as a tool and our profits as a resource to build the kingdom of God. So, as we grow and become more profitable the question now becomes, "What does God want us to do with the increase?" Sometimes it is very logical and sometimes it is something we would have never imagined.

CHAPTER TWO
POTENTIAL: DEVELOPMENT VERSUS DELIVERY

Consult not your fears, but your hopes and your dreams. Think not about your frustrations, but about your unfulfilled potential. Concern yourself not with what you tried and failed in, but with what it is still possible for you to do."– Pope John XXIII

And observe what the LORD your God requires: Walk in obedience to him, and keep his decrees and commands, his laws and regulations, as written in the Law of Moses. Do this so that you may prosper in all you do and wherever you go ....
— 1 Kings 2:3

Reaching Our Potential Means Dealing with Tension

Every time my wife and I go to a movie for a date night, there is tension. I want drama. She wants a light-hearted comedy. After five minutes in the car, we're debating (ok, fighting): What kind of date night is this? At the end of the night, we end up enjoying a good comedy.

Maybe you have tensions in your relationships, as well. Maybe you can't decide where to eat, Chinese or pizza? What soda to buy, Coke or Pepsi? What station to listen to, pop rock or oldies?

Obviously, we are starting with some light-hearted examples, but we know the bigger tensions in our life are very real. Tensions like:

How much to work vs. how much to be at home?

Do I spend or do I save in this season of life?

Should we send the kids to private school, public school, or homeschool?

In the business realm you may ask: Do I buy or sell? Do I aim for delivery or development? Is this a season to expand, take advantage of the downturn or to be ready when it goes up?

Both personally and professionally, the tensions never seem to lift. Furthermore it can be difficult to discern if the issue is actually a tension to be managed (because it's always going to be there) or if it's a problem to be solved (where there is a clear way out).[11]

So what about you? What are the biggest tensions in your life right now? Maybe you have teenagers at home and that creates tension. Maybe it's a really busy season at work, and that's the source.

God wants to break through your tensions and give you clarity in order to experience the abundant life he has promised you and all of us. This is what it takes to reach another level of our potential.

Business Tensions

Let's dig into this a bit. As we look at companies and organizations in the corporate and small business world, especially at the macro level, we will almost always find tension between *delivery* and *development*.

Delivery means profitability, execution and productivity. If we don't deliver, close the deal and make the sale, we aren't going to be able to grow, pay our employees and put food on the table. Quite simply, we have to deliver.

At the same time, we have to develop. As new products become old or dated, someone is always out there working to take our market share and woo our customers with newly developed products. So it can't only be about delivery—we also need development. Development is about infrastructure, innovation, training, ideas, experimentation, brainstorming, creativity, systems and processes. This framework helps us manage everything we're trying to deliver productively and efficiently. Businesses create whole HR departments and Six Sigma initiatives that help to develop products and services to be productive, efficient and profitable.

Intuitively, we know that if we get this rhythm of development and delivery right, we can better experience success and sustainable growth in our industry.

Managing this tension, though, is not as simple as this short explanation can make it sound, because tensions come with uncertainties. If we study our lives,

WE SEE THAT MOST PEOPLE ARE GOOD AT EITHER ONE OR THE OTHER— DELIVERY OR DEVELOPMENT.

and the lives of great leaders and leaders of the Bible like David, Moses and Paul, we see that most people are good at either one or the other—delivery or development. It takes trust, discernment and intentional effort to learn how to be someone who knows how to develop and how to deliver. It also takes a great deal of wisdom to personally and professionally discern the season, so you are able to act accordingly.

A Bite Out of the Apple

In October 2011 Steve Jobs, the mastermind behind Apple, passed away. If you have read any of his biographies or seen movies about him, you know that he had quite the life, with many highs and lows. Most of all, you see, he was a delivery guy. He was all about delivering the next product and the next innovation. In 1976, when he and his partner started Apple in his garage, he was passionate about the delivery of this product innovation, which continued throughout his life. This is what we loved about Jobs—his ability to deliver the next new thing.

In its infancy, Apple burst onto the scene. Jobs delivered at such a high level he had to bring in the president of Pepsi, John Sculley, to co-lead with him to develop the infrastructure of the company. Jobs originally convinced Sculley to leave Pepsi with the now-famous line: "Do you want to sell sugar water for the rest of your life, or do you want to come with me and change the world?"[12]

Jobs, a delivery guy, brought in a development guy, which inevitably created opportunity as well as tension. It's no surprise that this partner moved from being his best friend to his worst enemy. After Apple's second product released, Jobs said, "I want to deliver on the next computer," but his partner said, "No, we need to develop the current Apple II. We need to develop new software, new accessories, new opportunities to maximize this product." They went back and forth, and finally the decision went to the Apple board, which sided with the Pepsi guy, Sculley, and decided to develop, not deliver.

So Jobs left to start NeXT Computer and designed an amazing black desktop that was way overpriced and didn't do well in the market. At the same time he also bought George Lucas' division of a graphic design company that went on to create the most powerful operating system the world had ever seen. This design company's name? Pixar.

Meanwhile, as Jobs continued to deliver, the Apple development company slowly went downhill. Their operating system, Copland, was very mediocre. In a last ditch effort to survive, Apple bought NeXT Computer. Amazingly, when Apple bought Jobs' company, he became the de facto CEO of the company he was fired from, which meant that delivery and development were now back into one organization. Infrastructure met delivery, which meant new products with the structure to support them.

This started the real rise of Apple, and also created the rhythm of development and delivery that we now know so well. Every year there is going to be a new line of iPhones in late summer or fall, and every spring there will be a new iPad. Apple now has this rhythm of delivery and development down to a science. They are constantly innovating and delivering on those innovations, which is why we love Apple. The development/delivery tension is now a both/and rather than an either/or, and they work together to bring us new products year in and year out.

Now Back to You

To maximize our lives, not only from a business perspective, but also in our personal life, we need to think about these realities of delivery and development. It's part of understanding what it means to experience life to the full. As we stated earlier, none of us are perfect, and so everyone tends to have strength in delivery (make it happen, get things done) or development (creativity, ideas, infrastructure). As you can see in the matrix below, one without the other isn't good. However, with a level of self-awareness and intentional growth, everyone has the potential to balance them both in order to build a life and career that thrives.[13]

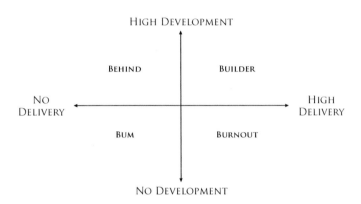

Of course this concept isn't a new one. Jesus described this tension as well, but he used the theological terminology of blessing and breakthrough. His desire is for us to have blessing in our lives—a life enjoyed to the full. Along with this blessing (development), Jesus also desires breakthrough (delivery).

Our observation is that some love to linger in the blessing, and some pioneer leaders love to constantly pursue breakthrough. These are not bad defaults, but one without the other can prove to be problematic.

If we focus only on blessing without breakthrough, we find ourselves merely indulging in the goodness of God. In that indulgence, we find ourselves missing out on the things he wants to expand into our lives, and we end up settling for seconds.

On the other hand, if we are all about breakthrough with no blessing, we find ourselves burnt out. Our lives will be defined by striving in constant work with no rest. We'll know how to plow new territory, but we won't learn how to enjoy it.

Lastly, if we focus on neither blessing nor breakthrough, we will go through life coasting or drifting, which is definitely not the life God calls us to.

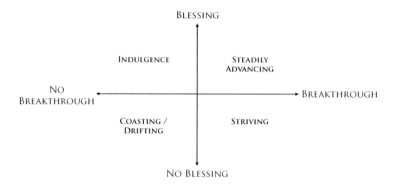

What we want to do is steadily advance—pressing forward in the kingdom (breakthrough) and continually going after Christ-likeness (blessing). A wise builder does both. Hearing and Doing. Blessing and Breakthrough. Development and Delivery.

Personally, I am more of a breakthrough guy. When I worked at Southland Christian Church in Lexington, Kentucky, I was all about pioneering discipleship, mission and leadership initiatives within the church. I was so focused on this that the leadership team I sat on eventually had to say, "You're moving too fast, pushing too hard, and when we start implementing, you're already onto the next thing."

They became skeptical of the pace of my leadership and the content that we were delivering. Because I pushed so much so fast, some dug their heels in, and we almost threw the baby out with the bathwater in terms of discipleship and mission. Even the people most loyal to me noticed the warning signs before I did.

Of course there were other complexities involved in the push for breakthrough, but looking back I see that my lack of self-awareness was a big part of the problem. Breakthrough people like me can often be so emphatic that we miss the signals like how little we're sleeping, the weight we're gaining, the obsessive stress we have, our inability to enjoy things and/or our inability to relax and rest.

An Example of Too Much Development

When I worked for Motorola outside of Glasgow, Scotland, I lived in a culture that was very cozy and indulgent—a hyper-development culture. At that time, the early 2000s, Motorola was on top of its game in many sectors, but they had become lax. They were all about development: a tweak here, a tweak there, and then releasing a "new" product for a higher price, even though not much had really changed. About the time I left Motorola, Samsung and Nokia innovated right past them, and Motorola caught on too late. They lingered too long in the blessing, and it got them in trouble. Even when Motorola realized this and ramped things up, they were too far behind their competitors, who were pumping out new phones and new technologies at a breakneck pace, especially in the European market. Even today, Motorola has had to innovate into other sectors and basically leave the cell phone business, because they were never able to catch up.

This can be a reality for churches, as well. Many expressions of the Christian Church do the same services and activities over and over, decade after decade, not seeing the subtle changes and shifts in culture, and not responding through new vehicles, attitudes and ways to be the church. At some point they realize their congregation is rapidly declining, with few to no newcomers coming through the doors. As they then reach out, they find the neighboring communities aren't interested. Yes, it's too late—the cheese has been moved.

An Example of Too Much Delivery

On the other hand, we don't want to be all delivery and be like the hundreds of dot-com companies that made millions of dollars delivering between 1999 and 2003, only to quickly lose all those millions when the stock market bubble burst. This was a delivery boom without any development or infrastructure behind it. Out of the 200+ dot-com companies with multimillion-dollar earnings during this boom, only three remain in business today—Amazon, eBay and Google.

This reality of development vs. delivery and of blessing vs. breakthrough is a big deal for us to think about if we want to reach our potential and go after all God has for us in life.

> **THEY KNOW HOW TO STEWARD THE BLESSING WELL, AND AT THE SAME TIME KNOW HOW TO GO AFTER BREAKTHROUGH.**

The best brands in the world get this right. Think about Apple, Coca-Cola or Chick-fil-A. They know how to steward the blessing well, and at the same time know how to go after breakthrough.

Which do you tend toward, blessing or breakthrough? Have you ever missed out on breakthrough because you focused too much on blessing? Have you ever missed out on blessing because you focused too much on breakthrough? What did you learn from these situations?

These are questions we must keep coming back to in order to continue to build on the life of abundance and fulfillment to which Jesus has called us.

Learning to Live It Out: Athlete, Soldier, Farmer, Engineer

One of my favorite qualities of the American culture is its history of pioneering, along with its continual pursuit of breakthrough, which the nation has mainly achieved through this grand experiment we call democracy.

Nothing captures this pioneering spirit better than the story of the 1893 Cherokee Outlet. This was the biggest land rush in the history of America. Thousands upon thousands of people lined up on the Midwestern border going into Louisiana, Oklahoma and Texas to try to claim more than 400,000 acres being released on a first-come, first-served basis. At noon on September 16, 1893, a gun fired, and pioneers rushed to stake their claim.[14] In order to get a piece of land, they needed to do two things: get there first and protect the land. These pioneers needed the skills of an athlete and a soldier. They needed the strength and speed to get ahead of the pack and literally stake their claim.

Fast forward one year later. We discover over 90 percent of the people who originally staked a claim had lost their land, because while they were great at getting there first and getting the breakthrough, they didn't know how to cultivate it. So just 12 months after the initial rush, the major land barons from New York and New England bought all this land for pennies on the dollar from the pioneers who didn't know how to cultivate the blessing. It was just like the dot-com bubble bursting, only 100 years earlier.

As we draw back to the Bible, we see these same metaphors taking place in 2 Timothy, as Paul neared the end of his life. This letter is like his last words—his last will and testament to his spiritual son, Timothy. Paul approached this letter by basically telling Timothy, "OK Tim, I've discipled you in so many things, as I have probably hundreds of disciples. Now the end is near, I'm going to pass away soon. And from this jail cell in Rome, I want to make sure all the tools in my leader bag get passed on to you. I don't want you to miss any of the essential leadership lessons I've gained over the course of my life. This letter is my essential leadership primer for you."

Here it is in the Scripture ...

You then, my son, be strong in the grace that is in Christ Jesus. And the things you have heard me say in the presence of many witnesses entrust to reliable people who will also be qualified to teach others. — 2 Timothy 2:1-2

Paul spent the rest of this chapter teaching Timothy to manage the tension between blessing and breakthrough, between one who delivers (a pioneer) and one who develops (a settler). To drive this home, Paul provided four metaphors: two for breakthrough and two for blessing.

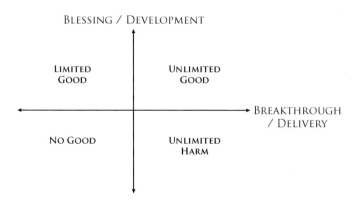

TO GET BREAKTHROUGH, YOU NEED THE SKILLS OF THE SOLDIER AND ATHLETE.

To get breakthrough, you need the skills of the Soldier and Athlete.

> Join with me in suffering, like a good soldier of Christ Jesus. No one serving as a soldier gets entangled in civilian affairs, but rather tries to please his commanding officer. Similarly, anyone who competes as an athlete does not receive the victor's crown except by competing according to the rules.
> — 2 Timothy 2:3-5

These are two metaphors Paul used in other letters as well. In Ephesians 6, he teaches us to put on the full armor of God. In 1 Corinthians 9, he talks about the athlete's skill, discipline and focus. Here Paul returned to these metaphors to summarize these essential skills Timothy would need to get breakthrough.

To live in the blessing, you need the skills of the Farmer and the Engineer.

Even if we are good at breakthrough, we also need to learn the skills of the farmer and the engineer that Paul talks about. These are skills the pioneers of the land rush definitely could have used!

TO LIVE IN THE BLESSING, YOU NEED THE SKILLS OF THE FARMER AND THE ENGINEER.

In the verses below, Paul echoed the metaphors of agriculture, farming, engineering and building which Jesus so often used. Paul summarized them here, talking about the hard worker (designer, engineer) as well as the farmer who is able to cultivate the breakthrough and enjoy the first fruits of that breakthrough in the form of blessing.

The hardworking farmer should be the first to receive a share of the crops. Reflect on what I am saying, for the Lord will give you insight into all this.
— 2 Timothy 2:6-7

Do your best to present yourself to God as one approved, a worker who does not need to be ashamed and who correctly handles the word of truth. Avoid godless chatter, because those who indulge in it will become more and more ungodly. — 2 Timothy 2:15-16

The juxtaposition of these four metaphors shows us that, if you want to be a leader who goes after everything God has for you, you have to know how to get the breakthrough and cultivate the blessing.

So have you identified your tendency yet? Is it indulgence over discipline (developer)? Or is it striving over rest (pioneer)? Take your time to discern your natural default in both your personal and professional life. Your greatest strengths overextended eventually become your weakness, and as we know, God's intent for you is a life of abundance. So spending time reflecting is well worth it.

PIONEER
- ▶ visionary
- ▶ restless
- ▶ entrepreneur
- ▶ dreamer
- ▶ inventor
- ▶ reformer
- ▶ risk-taker

SETTLER
- ▶ nurturer
- ▶ developer
- ▶ persevere
- ▶ endurance
- ▶ planter
- ▶ expand
- ▶ evolve

Getting Practical

Let's look at the mentalities of the athlete and the soldier to see what characteristics God may want us to grow in. Here's what we see in Scripture concerning the qualities of an athlete and a solider that are needed for breakthrough.

Athletes

- ▶ Athletes exercise incredible focus and discipline, and stay focused on the prize.[15]
- ▶ They have a clear goal and know what the win is. As a result, they can define and communicate the win to others.
- ▶ They exercise perseverance.
- ▶ They are focused on their individual responsibility, even in team sports.

Soldiers

- ▶ Soldiers understand that we are at war, that there is an enemy to fight and that real spiritual ground is at stake.[16]
- ▶ They know they need weapons, skills and competencies to help them achieve everything God is calling them to at home, marriage and at work.
- ▶ Soldiers have a communal mentality, as they know the devil seeks to kill, steal and destroy, and wants to isolate us.
- ▶ They know they have to band together and fight as one.[17]

In Summary: Pioneers / Delivery / Breakthrough

- ▶ Know the clear objective/defined win.
- ▶ Understand the importance of team and are responsible to every individual on that team.
- ▶ Know they need honed skills to get the victory.
- ▶ Have a strategic plan carried out through focus and discipline.

Now, let's think about what it looks like to cultivate the blessing, as we look at the mentality of the farmer and engineer.

Farmers

- ▶ Farmers are steady and consistent.
- ▶ They reflect in the offseason about what needs to change and how things can get better, which means they are constantly developing, refining and perfecting their craft.
- ▶ They know how to rest and reflect.
- ▶ They know what the harvest is and how to enjoy the blessing.

Engineers

▶ Engineers are hard workers who design, create and improve.

▶ They enjoy the work they create and the buildings they craft.

▶ They know how to be creative and are willing to be spontaneous.

▶ They don't feel bad about taking a day off to rest, reflect, indulge and also plan ahead.

▶ They ask what they need to do differently, in light of the past.

In Summary: Settlers / Development / Blessing

▶ Are steady and consistent.

▶ Can name and identify the blessing and know how to celebrate.

▶ Reflect on what can be done better.

▶ Are constantly improving and growing.

Application #1: Retreat to Advance, Discern the Season

Learning these skills starts with self-reflection as you grow into a greater level of self-awareness. The best way to accomplish this is through rest and reflection. This time is often referred to as a retreat. Jesus constantly retreated, and whenever he did, major revelation happened.

Harvard Business Review also recognizes the wisdom of retreats. One of their articles called it the *Shower Principle*. Basically, this states that most executives and CEOs have their best ideas in the shower.[18] Why in the world would this be? Well, it's because the shower is the only place they can reflect. Outside the shower, they are pulled in a million different directions. But in the shower they can't check their email, reply to texts or make phone calls. Their mind gets to rest for a few moments, and great ideas happen.

It's remarkable how much time we spend striving, even though our best

> IT'S REMARKABLE HOW MUCH TIME WE SPEND STRIVING, EVEN THOUGH OUR BEST IDEAS COME WHEN WE ARE AT REST.

ideas come when we are at rest. You would think this would cause us to retreat and reflect more, but we so quickly forget the value of retreating in order to develop ourselves as leaders, people and Christians. Instead we seem to have mastered the rhythm of work and collapse, work and collapse, and at the same time we wish we could come up with that next big thing. It's probably waiting for us on the back porch whenever we are ready to slow down and relax.

Yet on the other extreme, in a season of blessing, we can fall too far into resting and relaxing when focus and discipline are needed. After six weeks we've given up on our diet, given up on going to the gym and we've begun indulging instead of delivering. This kind of pattern won't lead to breakthrough.

Jesus Shows the Way

The disciples were constantly struggling with this tension. At times they pushed Jesus for another breakthrough, and Jesus had to remind them to rest in the blessing. At other times the disciples wanted to hang out and enjoy the blessing, but Jesus pushed them to move forward in the breakthrough.

In Mark 1:35, we see Jesus' response to this tension in his own life. After he had worked all day preaching, casting out demons, healing the sick and ministering to the poor, he encountered even more people who needed his assistance. So what did he do?

The verse says, "Late into the evening, he continued to minister to the people, but the next day, Jesus got up early to go out into the wilderness, and retreat from the crowd." He depended on the Father so much that he retreated after an exhausting day. He checked in with his Father and said, "Dad, what do you want me to do today?"

I think this is what God his Father told him: "Great job with the breakthrough yesterday. Now it's time for the blessing. Remember, you didn't come to heal everybody. You came to defeat the cross so everyone can be reconciled back to God. That's why you came. So in the midst of breakthrough, don't get all excited about yourself. Recalibrate. Think long term. Remember the big picture of why you're here, because if everyone in this town gets healed, but you are not able to defeat the cross, all is lost and the devil wins."

The Father was showing Jesus how to live in the tension, how to swing from one side to the other and how to live the abundant (not burnt-out) life to which he was called.

Back to the story in Mark 1, we see that when the disciples came and found Jesus spending time with the Father, they tried to lead him back to breakthrough, because an even larger crowd had gathered. The disciples wanted him to put on the healing and casting-out-demons show again. But Jesus told them that he had talked to his dad, and that the Father said they needed to go to other towns, as well. So they walked past the sick, the lepers and those desiring healing to go to the next town. The disciples wanted more breakthroughs, but because Jesus knew the wisdom of his Father, he did the counterintuitive thing and pursued blessing instead. So what happened to those poor people? Don't worry—in Mark 2 Jesus returned to an even larger crowd in this same town several days later, to heal more sick and cast out demons.

Compare that story with Matthew 17, when Jesus went up on the Mount of Transfiguration and took Peter, James and John with him. Jesus was transformed, and the Father in heaven spoke again to say, "This is my Son, whom I love; with him I am well pleased. Listen to him."[19] Moses and Elijah were even there. And what did Peter say? "Let's stay!" He wanted them to build some houses and stay a really long time. But Jesus told Peter not to build anything, because the blessing was over. Peter didn't realize it, but at the base of the mountain the disciples were trying and failing to cast out a demon. Jesus, Peter, James and John needed to go down the mountain and go for the breakthrough. The disciples at the base of the mountain were prophesying in Jesus' name, but they couldn't cast out the demon. Jesus' further instruction on breakthrough was needed.

In Summary

We want to be leaders who get excited about the opportunity to build something significant in and through our lives, yet we also want to be leaders who realize that we must adhere to necessary seasons if we want to see the maximum level of kingdom impact. We don't want to be like Motorola, enjoying unprecedented success for a while only to burn out within 15 years or so. Many business leaders face this burnout, even after five years. We want to be like Jesus, who conquered sin and death all the way through the final battle. We want to be like Paul, who at 70 years old was still assuredly running toward the finish line.

Application #2: Gas, Brakes, and Steering

Are you in a season where you are going uphill? Is it a breakthrough time? If so, it's about steering (keeping the vision calibrated and on track) and pushing the pedal to the metal (pushing the vision forward). If you slow down on the way up, you may never regain the momentum to ultimately get to the top.

Or is it a season *after* some big breakthroughs? Maybe you're at the top of the hill, and now it's time to go downhill. If so, you need steering and brakes, so you can rest and enjoy the ride. If you try to hit the gas going downhill, you're going to end up in a wreck. We all know lots of business leaders who've made this mistake.

The devil is really clever. He will get you working hard in seasons of blessing, and he'll enjoy seeing you exhausted in times where there needs to be a breakthrough. That's how he works, and if you don't discern where you are on the hill, your breakthroughs and blessings will be few and far between.

So what season are you in right now? Is this a season where you need to retreat and develop a sense of clarity? Maybe God wants to bless you with a season of abiding and revelation. Reap the benefits like the farmer and the engineer. Are there some weekends he wants you to engage with close friends, hear from him and enjoy the blessing of others in your life?

Or maybe you have some clarity, you know what you are called to build and you know what the next season needs to look like. You just need courage to pick up the tools of the athlete and the soldier and to believe you can do all things through Christ who gives you strength.[20]

So in the meantime, when you aren't wrestling over the tension of Coke or Pepsi, allow the bigger tensions in your life to ignite what God is building in and around you. In doing so, you'll be able to take your personal and professional life to the next level so you can live the abundant life he promises!

As it turns out, Star Trek's Mr. Spock had it right when he said, *"Live Long (Development / Blessing) and Prosper (Delivery / Breakthrough)!"*

You don't have to prosper only to burn out, and you don't have to live long only to miss it.

You can do both!

Discussion Questions

1.   What is the biggest tension in your life right now—personally and professionally?

2.   Which do you tend toward, delivery/blessing or developing/breakthrough?

3.   Have you ever missed out on breakthrough because you focused on blessing? Have you ever missed out on blessing because you focused too much on breakthrough? What did you learn from those situations?

4.   Is your tendency indulgence over discipline (developer)? Or is it striving over

rest (pioneer)? How can you better balance these tendencies?

5.   What season are you in right now? Where are you on the hill? What needs to happen for you to engage and rightly adjust to the season you are in?

Putting It Into Practice

Cory Carlson: President of Sales at URETEK Holdings, Inc.
The tension between development and delivery is a work in progress as I develop in my leadership and faith. Brandon and the Five Capitals team were instrumental in helping me through this process as I recently underwent a key career transition. My natural tendency leans toward a pioneer, where I get involved in an endeavor, spend time to get the ball moving, get some early wins and then move on to the next thing. I don't know if I am a pioneer because of the adrenaline rush of starting something new, or because of fear of being stagnant in the same role. However, as I grow in my faith, I realize the season of settling is necessary, not only in the development of my team, but also in my relationship with God.

My most recent transition was becoming president of sales for a company where over the last 18 months we have added 50 percent of the sales force and trained the new and existing team. Brandon and I worked on pushing the team toward leading on their own, so they were all in delivery mode; however, we also knew it would take time to develop them. This development period was critical to the team as they grew in our company values of accountability and development. During this time, our team was not the only one growing. I was also growing as I realized the importance of settling and abiding in God. Although I have been anxious to add additional product lines or move certain team members to new roles, I realize I need to remain in this development season. This abiding time has caused me to pause, pray and get clarity on what our next steps will be as a team when we are ready to transition to the next phase.

CHAPTER THREE
PARADIGM SHIFT:
THE RIGHT INVESTMENTS

He is no fool who gives what he cannot keep to gain what he cannot lose.[21]
— Jim Elliot

**Well done, good and faithful servant! You have been faithful with a few things;
I will put you in charge of many things. Come and share your master's happiness!
— *1 Kings 2:3***

Have Your Cake and Eat It Too

More money, more problems.

This was certainly the case for William Post III in 1988 when he won $16.2 million in the Pennsylvania lottery. He thought all his problems were over. Instead he almost instantly encountered crime, bankruptcy, tragedy and incredibly poor spending habits. Within the first two weeks, he had already purchased a restaurant, a used-car lot and an airplane. His careless spending continued, and within three months he was $500,000 in debt.

Money seemed to be the least of his problems, however, as days later the news reported that Post's brother had been arrested for hiring a hit man to try to kill William and his sixth wife. Yes, you read that correctly—his sixth wife. Other relatives and friends convinced him to invest his money into worthless business opportunities and a landlady tricked him into giving her a third of his cash. More money *did* equal more problems for Post.

In 1993, Post said, "Everybody dreams of winning money, but nobody realizes the nightmares that come out of the woodwork, or the problems." Like the time he was jailed for firing a gun at a bill collector. Obviously his winnings did little to improve his life, and at one point he allegedly claimed, "I was much happier when I was broke."[22] At age 66, Post died of respiratory failure, leaving behind his seventh wife and nine children from his second marriage.

Sadly, stories like Post's are all too familiar. When we think about lottery winners going broke, we know the appropriate reaction is to say that the good life isn't just about money, yet at the same time we know God hasn't intended for us to the live life from paycheck to paycheck.

Since money is the second most talked about topic in the Bible (after his kingdom), we can trust that God clearly wants to engage with us on the topic of money and how we interact with it.

My Story

Alongside my fraternity brothers at Iowa State, I worked hard my senior year to secure the best possible job, hoping to set myself up for a great career and life. I networked with key alumni, researched the top companies, discerned the best overall job opportunities and aggressively worked to get an interview. Initially (and maybe a bit naively) I assumed I would be one of the few to secure a great job during the fall of my senior year, which would ensure an easy final eight months during which I would coast my way to graduation.

By Thanksgiving, no job. By Valentines Day, no job.

Finally, my dream job came through with Eli Lilly and Company in Indianapolis, Indiana, working in their animal health marketing division, Elanco. Full of myself and my American Dream mentality, I bought an expensive house and an expensive car within the first year of moving to Indiana. While the job was great and I worked with many fantastic people, the first three months were a brutal wake-up call. I didn't know anyone. I'd left all my friends and networks in Iowa, I had no church home and I had no knowledge of the area. I was beginning to wonder if the highest salary offer I'd received was worth the move across three states. I had left behind what I know now to be one of the keys to a fulfilling life—
community.

Of course God was gracious as he eventually provided a church home and gave me friends through work and in my neighborhood. I was even blessed to find a fantastic friend and work mentor, Kelly, who navigated me through the complexities of corporate life. In short, God got me there. Looking back, however, I might have done some things differently.

What's Really Missing

We could all describe scenarios in our own life or in the lives of those we know that are related to the paths followed in the stories above. Maybe a dad who works such long hours his kids barely know him. Or a friend whose relationship with his wife becomes more distant every time he cancels plans with her for some "very important" task at work. Or even a local executive who makes the evening news when agents of the FBI and IRS show up to search his home and office.

Again and again, we see those who seem to be on the path to having it all end up with hardly anything. So what are we missing? What exactly is this good life we are after, and what do our priorities need to be in order to achieve this elusive good life?

God has hard-wired us with a desire to seek a healthy, more fulfilling life. Naturally, we pursue happiness, goodness, abundance and health. When we get sick, we do everything we can to get better. When we move into a new house, we seek to make the living spaces comfortable. We eat food that tastes good. We heat our homes in the winter. We want our children to be set up for success in life. We seek meaningful friendships and want a stable and happy home life with our immediate family. After all, nobody makes New Year's resolutions to eat more junk food, become a worse friend or be more in debt.

But is life to the full really the same as having it all?

Ever feel like something's missing?

You might recall the encounter Jesus had with a rich young ruler. The ruler had money, power and youth. He was also righteous, meaning that he held to the expectations of Jewish law. In the eyes of any first-century Jew, this man had it all.

And yet he came to Jesus asking what more he needed to do to "inherit eternal life." We can assume that eternal life not only meant unending life, but also a flourishing, abundant life here and now.

This is the heartache the rich young ruler felt that drove him to ask Jesus this question. Despite the ruler's riches, power and good standing with the community, he recognized something in Jesus that he didn't have; some kind of abundance that he couldn't access. Here's exactly what happened:

> As Jesus started on his way, a man ran up to him and fell on his knees before him. "Good teacher," he asked, "what must I do to inherit eternal life?"
> "Why do you call me good?" Jesus answered. "No one is good—except God alone. You know the commandments: 'You shall not murder, you shall not commit adultery, you shall not steal, you shall not give false testimony, you shall not defraud, honor your father and mother.'"
> "Teacher," he declared, "all these I have kept since I was a boy."
> Jesus looked at him and loved him. "One thing you lack," he said. "Go, sell everything you have and give to the poor, and you will have treasure in heaven. Then come, follow me."
> At this the man's face fell. He went away sad, because he had great wealth.
> Jesus looked around and said to his disciples, "How hard it is for the rich to enter the kingdom of God!"
> The disciples were amazed at his words. But Jesus said again, "Children, how hard it is to enter the kingdom of God! It is easier for a camel to go through the eye of a needle than for someone who is rich to enter the kingdom of God."
> The disciples were even more amazed, and said to each other, "Who then can be saved?"
> Jesus looked at them and said, "With man this is impossible, but not with God; all things are possible with God." — Mark 10:17-27

We often think that Jesus was being overly harsh with the rich young ruler. After all, liquidating his riches didn't seem to be an entrance requirement for anyone else. Does it mean we all need to sell our possessions? Is it wrong to be rich? How much money counts as "rich," we nervously wonder.

But the reality is that Jesus wasn't being harsh with the rich young ruler. He was actually offering him the opportunity of a lifetime—a chance to inherit eternal life and truly have it all.

Jesus' strange and shocking answer to the rich young ruler was *not* to tell him he shouldn't seek the good life. Jesus' answer was basically to offer the rich young ruler an internship in which he would learn how to live the good life. It would cost him everything, but Jesus said the young ruler could have it all, and that it was appropriate to seek this goal.

> # THE SAME OFFER IS EXTENDED TO US, BUT TO ACCEPT IT, WE MUST RECALIBRATE OUR IDEA OF WHAT IT MEANS TO HAVE IT ALL.

The same offer is extended to us, but to accept it, we must recalibrate our idea of what it means to have it all. Typically we define the good life too narrowly and look for it in all the wrong places. Our searching leads us to disappointment time and time again, and all the while Jesus is beckoning us to experience his good, full and abundant life!

Warren Buffett once said, "Never invest in a business you can't understand."

As a businessman and former corporate employee, I know the wisdom in this statement. Usually the number one concern of any business can be boiled down to these four words: *Show me the money*. Those involved and making an investment in the company want and need to understand the bottom line. How will they make a profit, how will they meet their investors' expectations and ultimately, how will they become wealthy?

In our society, wealth typically refers to financial assets and worldly possessions, and names like Donald Trump, Bill Gates or Mark Zuckerberg come to mind—individuals who have accumulated an enormous amount of financial success. Such success is what many of us dream about and aspire to. We wish we could experience just an ounce of their good fortune.

Yet as we dig into the root meaning of the word wealth, we see it comes from an old Middle English word that simply means "well-being." And it's true wealth that goes beyond financial investments in mutual funds or stocks and rather addresses the everyday, normal fundamentals of economics, capital and investment.

It's about how we manage our lives and how we invest our capital (time, resources, relationships, etc.) to follow Jesus and see his kingdom break in and transform people's lives. It's not just about me flourishing—it's about our whole family, community and co-workers flourishing. It's about the common good, not just our individual prosperity.

It's in this context that our definition is redefined and we begin to find true life in all the right places.

This is true wealth.

The Right Lens of Investment

Jesus talked about the good life in the Sermon on the Mount. In this instance, he showed us how to seek it: "Do not worry about your life, what you will eat or drink, or your body, what you will wear .... But seek first his kingdom and his righteousness, and all these things will be given to you as well."[23]

This is an astonishing invitation and one of the best how-to guides you could ever ask for. Jesus is saying, "If you follow me, you can safely stop worrying about these things." People who don't know God are the ones who run after these things and worry about them, but your Father in heaven knows you need them, and he will care for you.

Here's another way to say it: "If you make it your top priority to be involved in what God is doing and have his goodness increasingly fill your life, everything else will be taken care of."

When you're aiming at the target, pursuing the most valuable thing, then you're living abundantly *and* you've inherited eternal life.

HIS KINGDOM

The rich young ruler may have felt like Jesus was being extra hard on him, but Jesus wasn't asking him to do anything different from what he asked his 12 disciples to do. Peter and Andrew as well as James and John left their nets and followed Jesus. Matthew quit his job as a tax collector and forfeited a lucrative career to follow Jesus. This didn't mean they simply left their nets in the garage or closed the tax booth for the weekend. The disciples left their only means of supporting themselves. Fishing and tax collecting were their businesses, their livelihood, so leaving their nets and ledgers meant quitting their jobs and ending their careers. It was a big deal!

Unfortunately this is often how we hear and how discipleship is often preached—through the lens of sacrifice (what we lose). But Jesus rarely spoke this way! When Jesus talked about discipleship, he always spoke through the lens of investment by looking at what we gain. He promised people that what initially looks and feels like a sacrifice will pay off in the end, which is the same thing as making a good investment.

Here are a few more verses that emphasize the power of making decisions through the lens of investment.

> **WHEN JESUS TALKED ABOUT DISCIPLESHIP, HE ALWAYS SPOKE THROUGH THE LENS OF INVESTMENT BY LOOKING AT WHAT WE GAIN.**

Whoever finds their life will lose it, and whoever loses their life for my sake will find it. — Matthew 10:39

The kingdom of heaven is like treasure hidden in a field. When a man found it, he hid it again, and then in his joy went and sold all he had and bought that field. — Matthew 13:44

And everyone who has left houses or brothers or sisters or father or mother or wife or children or fields for my sake will receive a hundred times as much and will inherit eternal life.
— Matthew 19:29

What's striking about these and other passages is the promise of a return on the investment. It's not just a call to lose your life because it's the right thing to do or because it's what God wants. It's a promise that you'll actually find real new life if you will only let go of the old one. It's the deal of a lifetime—a free upgrade and an investment that yields a return!

When I became a Christian my sophomore year at Iowa State, the sacrifices of letting go of my old life to enter into this new life with Jesus were very real. No more crazy party nights, a change in my choice of language and an overall reorienting of my priorities were just a few the adjustments I made.

WHAT'S STRIKING ABOUT THESE AND OTHER PASSAGES IS THE PROMISE OF A RETURN ON THE INVESTMENT.

In the midst of these changes, I experienced love, hope and contentment like never before, which far outweighed these sacrifices. I won't lie and say I did this without struggle, but my life had awakened to a new sense of purpose and I was enjoying the quality of my daily investments that yielded a return of a good, abundant life.

The Economics of Jesus

To be sure, the journey of seeking first his kingdom and learning to invest in the right things in life isn't always easy—and certainly hasn't been a one-and-done process for me. I am growing in it every day and learning how to be the hero in the stories he gives me: A hero who takes risks, invests wisely and consequently experiences life abundantly, both personally, professionally and spiritually. A hero who sees life through the lens of investment, in order that my return is greater than I could ever ask or imagine.

These are the kind of heroes Jesus is longing for and the ones the Bible talks about. As I dig into the Bible, I am challenged to identify those individuals Jesus called heroes—those who invested in the right things and sought his kingdom above everything else, and yet were still the unlikely heroes *and villains* of the Bible.

The story of the Good Samaritan is a great example of heroes and villains you might not expect. In fact, in Jesus' day even the term "Good Samaritan" would have been a laughable oxymoron! Everyone *knew* Samaritans weren't good, which makes Jesus' story all the more explosive.

Here's how it goes: A man is robbed and beaten to near death along a dangerous road. A priest who happens to be walking along the same road sees the man lying there, but passes by on the other side of the road. A worker in the temple comes across the man and does the same thing. Finally a good-for-nothing Samaritan sees the man and becomes the unlikely hero of the story by bandaging the man's wounds, carrying him to an inn and paying for his recovery. The priest and the Levite, whom everyone expected to be the heroes turned out to be the villains, while the expected villain turned out to be the hero. Jesus often used such juxtaposition in his stories, and it made a lot of people angry with him.

One of the most interesting and disturbing features of the villains of Jesus' stories is how *normal* and *ordinary* they are—which makes us deeply uncomfortable. Jesus told another story, a parable in fact, about kingdom economics. See if you can identify who the villain of the story will be.

> Again, it will be like a man going on a journey, who called his servants and entrusted his wealth to them. To one he gave five bags of gold, to another two bags, and to another one bag, each according to his ability. Then he

went on his journey. The man who had received five bags of gold went at once and put his money to work and gained five bags more. So also the one with two bags of gold gained two more. But the man who had received one bag went off, dug a hole in the ground, and hid his master's money.

After a long time, the master of those servants returned and settled accounts with them. The man who had received five bags of gold brought the other five. "Master," he said, "you entrusted me with five bags of gold. See, I have gained five more."

His master replied, "Well done, good and faithful servant! You have been faithful with a few things; I will put you in charge of many things. Come and share your master's happiness!"

The man with two bags of gold also came. "Master," he said, "you entrusted me with two bags of gold; see, I have gained two more."

His master replied, "Well done, good and faithful servant! You have been faithful with a few things; I will put you in charge of many things. Come and share your master's happiness!"

Then the man who had received one bag of gold came. "Master," he said, "I knew that you are a hard man, harvesting where you have not sown and gathering where you have not scattered seed. So I was afraid and went out and hid your gold in the ground. See, here is what belongs to you."

His master replied, "You wicked, lazy servant! So you knew that I harvest where I have not sown and gather where I have not scattered seed? Well then, you should have put my money on deposit with the bankers, so that when I returned I would have received it back with interest.

"So take the bag of gold from him and give it to the one who has ten bags. For whoever has will be given more, and they will have abundance. Whoever does not have, even what they have will be taken from them. And throw that worthless servant outside, into the darkness, where there will be weeping and gnashing of teeth." — Matthew 25:14-30

Jesus did something in this parable that he did frequently—he used an economic image to talk about the kingdom of God and reveal a frame of reference that helps us understand our life.

Again, from our vantage point, what the master says seems astonishingly harsh:

"You wicked, lazy servant!" He gives the poor servant a severe tongue-lashing, takes his money away, and throws him out into the darkness, "where there will be weeping and gnashing of teeth."

Honestly, I look at that poor guy and think, "He doesn't seem so bad! All he did was nothing." But as we've said, Jesus' villains are very normal, and this disturbs us because we begin to see ourselves in the story. We think doing nothing would be better than trying to invest and losing everything, but for Jesus losing everything on a bad investment would have been better than doing nothing.

FOR JESUS LOSING EVERYTHING ON A BAD INVESTMENT WOULD HAVE BEEN BETTER THAN DOING NOTHING.

This servant wasn't *trying* to be a villain, but because he lacked trust in his master and had a scarcity mentality, he refused to invest the money. He assumed that failure in investment would be met with punishment, and thus remained passive. He is an unlikely, accidental villain, but a villain nonetheless, because he didn't cooperate with the master's investment plan.

Unfortunately it is easy to become an accidental villain. Think about the 2008 housing bubble and worldwide financial crisis of the early 2000s. A few *intentional villains* knew they were gaming the system and making money at other people's expense, but most people were accidental villains who got caught up in the hype of trying to make money off an exotic new financial product, inadvertently contributing to a system that caused many people to lose their homes and life savings.

Other people are villains because they intentionally invest in bad things for selfish reasons. Still other people end up as villains because they don't invest in the right things, like the third servant in Jesus' parable.

Jesus' stories teach us that heroes *intentionally invest* in the right things, to

> **JESUS' STORIES TEACH US THAT HEROES *INTENTIONALLY INVEST* IN THE RIGHT THINGS, TO LEVERAGE EVERYTHING ON BEHALF OF WHAT REALLY MATTERS.**

leverage everything on behalf of what really matters. Once again this is just another way of saying, "Seek first the kingdom of God, and all these things will be given to you as well."

So this way, even if we do win the lottery like William Post, III, our hearts will be aligned with our Father, so that every investment after that will be in the right things.

This is the full, abundant life Jesus promises us, and the best investment, which yields true wealth.

This is the life in which we become the hero of our own story.

This is a life worth building, and this is how we build a better life.

Discussion Questions

1. What does a flourishing, abundant life mean to you? What does it look like long-term and in your day-to-day life, both at work and home?

2. What kinds of things have you typically invested in to achieve the good life? Kids' activities? Job promotions? Living near family? Have you found these things to be the right places or the wrong places?

3. Do you really believe that if you seek first the kingdom, which means making it your top priority to be involved in what God is doing, everything else will be taken care of?

4. What was your reaction to Jesus' stories that depict normal and ordinary people as the villains of the story? Who did you most identify with and what did you learn from his definitions of investment?

5. Jesus teaches us that heroes intentionally invest in the right things. What things do you sense God is encouraging you to intentionally invest in?

Putting It Into Practice

Melissa Rogers, MD

One of my favorite verses is Deuteronomy 30:15, where we find the Israelite people on the brink of entering the Promised Land. As they sat in anticipation, God had Moses remind the people, "I have put before you life and prosperity ... death and destruction. Now, choose life." (paraphrase) Choosing life is hard sometimes. The world tells us that life is in success, money, popularity, etc., and like everyone else I knew, I was pursuing the same things. I graduated in the top of my college class, so I got a scholarship to medical school (because I could). I graduated in the top of my medical school class, so I decided to practice neurosurgery (because I could). Looking back, I'm not sure I ever asked God what life meant from his perspective. I was just pursuing the American Dream. I had money, respect, opportunity and more of the same ahead of me.

Then one day, in the dark hallway of a hospital, after seeing yet another young baby die from shaken baby syndrome, I realized this pursuit was killing me. I had my priorities upside down. I was pursuing financial and intellectual capital, but couldn't remember the last time I had pursued God or friends. I was too busy for church, too busy for family or friends, and physically I was exhausted. It was in that moment I decided to "seek first the Kingdom of God" and trust that everything else would come. Within six weeks of that dark hallway moment, I had resigned my residency, my house was on the market and I was on active duty in the military and on my way to my first assignment in south Georgia. At my going-away party, one of the most successful people I know (in terms of the world's description) told me, "You have discovered sooner than I that there is more to life than this." He too was disillusioned, but didn't have the courage to change. He is still in that job to this day. He has chosen death.

Choosing life has not been easy, but time has proven God's promise to be true. Several years ago my husband and I developed our family mission statement, which has brought us amazing clarity about the things we are going to do with our one and only life. Our mission is "To bring Peace, Healing and Wholeness in Jesus' name." Though all those things are counter to cultural pursuits, our life is much more full, enjoyable, balanced and productive than it ever was pursuing money, prestige, security and success. The question still rings true: What does it profit a man (or a business) if he gains the world ... but loses his soul? Choose life!

CHAPTER FOUR
PRIORITIES:
THE FIVE CAPITALS

We don't drift in good directions. We discipline and prioritize ourselves there.
– Allen Klein

But seek first his kingdom and his righteousness,
and all these things will be given to you as well.
– John 14:6

Five Kinds of Capital

As you think over your life, what kinds of capital has God invested in you? What skills and attributes has he grown into you over the years? Have you taken advantage of these? Are you using them? Are they producing a return for you and your family?

One capital God has invested in me over the years is *intellectual capital*. Unfortunately as an undergrad at Iowa State, I squandered a big portion of this investment. I picked agricultural business as one of my majors, but for all the wrong reasons. Sure, it got me into the fraternity I wanted to join and ensured all my classes were with my friends, but I had zero interest in the coursework. Had it not been for good study partners (and additional majors I was passionate about), I could have easily flunked out. Later in life, getting a master's degree in biblical studies from Asbury Seminary was a lot different. I was excited about the material, self-motivated and able to apply the content directly to my work. This investment is still paying out dividends today.

Now I can look back and clearly see God's investment of intellectual capital all over my life—and also other kinds of capital he is growing in me each and every day.

The word capital is defined as: *wealth in the form of money or other assets owned by a person or organization—available for a particular purpose such as starting a company or investing.*[24]

God has invested so much in us. He desires that we grow his investment and give it away, believing a greater return will come back to us only to then be invested in again. Building on the parable of the talents that we discussed in the previous chapter, my Five Capitals team and I believe there are Five Capitals from heaven available to us, and that there's a correct order to these capitals. If we keep them in order, grow them and give them away, we will experience a return on these investments. Then we will hear God's words: "Well done, good and faithful servant! You have been faithful with a few things; I will put you in charge of many things. Come and share your master's happiness!"[25]

The story of the shrewd manager helps to illustrate these Five Capitals and the importance of keeping them prioritized.

> Jesus told his disciples: "There was a rich man whose manager was accused of wasting his possessions. So he called him in and asked him, "What is this I hear about you? Give an account of your management, because you cannot be manager any longer."
>
> "The manager said to himself, 'What shall I do now? My master is taking away my job. I'm not strong enough to dig, and I'm ashamed to beg—I know what I'll do so that when I lose my job here, people will welcome me into their houses.'
>
> "So he called in each one of his master's debtors. He asked the first, 'How much do you owe my master?'
>
> "'Nine hundred gallons of olive oil,' he replied.
>
> "The manager told him, 'Take your bill, sit down quickly, and make it four hundred and fifty.'
>
> "Then he asked the second, 'And how much do you owe?'

"'A thousand bushels of wheat,' he replied.

"He told him, 'Take your bill and make it eight hundred.'

"The master commended the dishonest manager because he had acted shrewdly. For the people of this world are more shrewd in dealing with their own kind than are the people of the light. I tell you, use worldly wealth to gain friends for yourselves, so that when it is gone, you will be welcomed into eternal dwellings.

"Whoever can be trusted with very little can also be trusted with much, and whoever is dishonest with very little will also be dishonest with much. So if you have not been trustworthy in handling worldly wealth, who will trust you with true riches? And if you have not been trustworthy with someone else's property, who will give you property of your own?

"No one can serve two masters. Either you will hate the one and love the other, or you will be devoted to the one and despise the other. You cannot serve both God and money." — Luke 16:1-13

Reading this parable jars me a bit. I get that last part about not serving God and money, but what's with the sneaky behavior of the dishonest manager being *commended* by the master? Talk about unlikely heroes and villains.

Jesus seems to distill the parable into a pithy statement that sums up its main message. (Nowadays he could have tweeted it!) When Jesus says, "You cannot serve both God and money," he is saying that we can have only one ultimate point of reference—one ultimate priority. Eventually, the thing we value highest will win out, whether that is God or money.

He was telling his listeners that their method of assigning value to the elements of the world around them was way off. In short, this entire parable is about *how to value various forms of capital in order to invest wisely*.

Right off the bat, we see Jesus identify two forms of capital. They are *financial capital* (money) and what we call *spiritual capital* (God, or more specifically, our relationship or connection with God as a disciple of Christ).

Over and over in this parable and in all his other teachings, Jesus shows us that spiritual capital is not only different from financial capital, but far more valuable.[26] He has to make this point repeatedly because the world around him had it backwards. Like us, they tended to value financial capital above everything else. They also *equated* financial capital with spiritual capital—the general assumption of the day was that if you were rich it was a sure sign of God's favor on your life. This perspective caused them to make bad investments. This same perspective lingers today.

As we move further into the text we begin to see other forms of capital.

When the manager realizes he is about to be fired, he begins to think about what to do next. During his thought process he says, "I'm not strong enough to dig." Here he is contemplating one possible way of gaining financial capital after he loses his job—manual labor. We call this *physical capital*, the amount of time and energy we have available to invest. The shrewd manager realized that he had very little of this capital to invest (not being strong enough to dig, after all) and therefore decided it wasn't a great option for him.

After contemplating his situation, the manager says, "I know what I'll do." He thinks of a brilliant idea, one he is later praised for by his master (which is why this is the parable of the shrewd manager). The manager's shrewdness is actually another form of capital—*intellectual capital*. Intellectual capital refers to the ideas, knowledge and creativity we have to invest. The manager used his capacity to think creatively (his intellectual capital) to think of an idea for how to survive after he lost his job.

We see the final capital in this passage in the idea the manager comes up with. He uses the last few hours of his authority over his master's financial capital to reduce the debt that several people owed his master. The manager reasoned that this would allow him to be welcomed into their homes after he lost his job. In reducing their debt, he was gaining what we call *relational capital* with them. He leveraged his *intellectual capital* by investing *financial capital* in order to grow *relational capital*.

The master recognizes the wisdom in this move (even though the manager was scheming with his money) because the manager invests financial, intellectual and physical capital to gain relational capital. Jesus says this is a great investment. Jesus actually says it quite bluntly, "Use worldly wealth to gain friends for yourselves."

Many of us wrestle with this verse. Was Jesus really counseling us to buy friends? In fact, I think he was! Jesus is

JESUS IS SAYING IT IS WORTH INVESTING YOUR FINANCIAL CAPITAL TO GROW YOUR RELATIONAL CAPITAL, BECAUSE RELATIONAL CAPITAL IS WORTH FAR MORE THAN FINANCIAL CAPITAL.

saying it is worth investing your financial capital to grow your relational capital, because relational capital is worth far more than financial capital. That's the punch line of the parable. Jesus tells us to use our money to invest in people's lives so that we get friendship out of it. In other words, recognize the relative value of each kind of capital and invest wisely.

So, altogether we've identified five capitals: *financial* (the most tangible and highly valued by most people), *spiritual* (actually the most valuable), *physical* (apparently somewhere in the middle), *intellectual* (creative ideas) and *relational* (investment in people).

1. Spiritual Capital

How much **spiritual equity** do we have to invest?

▶ The currency is wisdom and power.

2. Relational Capital

How much **relational equity** do we have to invest?

▶ The currency is family and friends.

3. Physical Capital

How much **time and energy** do we have to invest?

▶ The currency is hours and health.

4. Intellectual Capital

How much **creativity and knowledge** do we have to invest?

▶ The currency is insight and ideas.

5. Financial Capital

How much **treasure** do we have to invest?

▶ The currency is money: dollars and cents, pounds and pennies, etc.

When the order and flow of these capitals are off, our lives are off. We see this fight for order throughout the entire Bible, as people made wise or poor investments based on gaining certain kinds of capital.

- ▶ Adam and Eve gave away their relational capital with God for intellectual capital— "knowing good and evil."
- ▶ Abraham left his family (relational capital) to obey God, going to the new land God had called him to (spiritual capital), letting Lot take the better land (financial capital) and being rewarded for it.
- ▶ Peter left his nets (the financial capital of his livelihood) to follow Jesus (spiritual capital). Matthew did the same with his livelihood of tax collecting.
- ▶ King Saul was chosen because of an abundance of physical capital (he was tall and handsome), while King David, his successor, had an abundance of spiritual capital. Saul ended his kingly career in ruin, while David is considered Israel's greatest king.

These are just a few examples, but I challenge you to read other stories and see if you can identify the kinds of investments that are made and the order in which people prioritized the capitals.

Remember the words of Warren Buffet: "Never invest in a business you can't understand." Once again this is wise advice. So as we move forward in these Five Capitals, we want to make sure we understand the process of how God's kingdom views them. Here we will look at each capital in more depth to see what it is, how it functions, what its currency is, how to invest it and how to grow it. We'll start with the most valuable (spiritual), and follow in the descending order.

Spiritual Capital

Spiritual capital is a way of talking about the level of connection (or intimacy) we have with God. Hence the first commandment: "You should love the Lord your God with all your heart, soul, and strength." This results in a kind of *spiritual equity* that we can invest in others. The currency of spiritual capital is *wisdom and power*, which comes from creating the space to hear from God and responding with faith and obedience.

> # WISDOM IS WHERE KNOWLEDGE AND LOVE COMBINE, AND POWER IS SIMPLY OPERATING IN CHRIST'S AUTHORITY WITH HIS RESOURCES.

Jesus carried more spiritual capital than any other human being, before or since. It was infinite and came from his constant connection with his dad. When people tried to praise *him*, he'd say things like: "the Father and I are one" and "I only do what I see the Father doing." The two things that people around him were constantly amazed at were his *teaching*, which reflected a large store of wisdom that he shared, and his *miracles*, which reflected the great amount of power that flowed through his life. When we grow in spiritual capital, we grow in wisdom and power. Wisdom is where knowledge and love combine, and power is simply operating in Christ's authority with his resources.

According to Jesus, *spiritual capital* is the most valuable of all. It is more important than relational capital, physical capital, intellectual capital and financial capital. This is clear from the entire ministry of Jesus. When Jesus talked about life in the kingdom of God, he talked about a life that was rich in spiritual capital. And when Jesus talked about eternal life, he wasn't talking just about long-lasting life—he was talking about a life rich in spiritual capital here and now on earth, as well as forever.

Is this level of wisdom and power really available to us? Of course—that's why God sent his one and only son. So we might be reconciled back to God—to grow in this oneness—in this capital. This is why Jesus can confidently say: "You can do everything I can do and even greater things than these."[27] The kingdom of God and eternal life are like code words that refer to a life filled with spiritual capital.

Relational Capital

Relational capital is how much *relational equity* we have to invest. The currency of relational capital is *family and friends*.

Relational capital comes in at number two on the list. Intuitively, this makes sense: love God (spiritual capital); love people (relational capital). Relational capital refers to the quantity and quality of our relationships with others. It's about how healthy and productive those relationships are. Having family and friends is incredibly valuable. The amount of relational capital we have benefits us and others in multiple ways, from our overall sense of well-being and happiness to more tangible realities. For instance, if you lose your job and get kicked out of your apartment (to use an extreme example), you'd better have some friends and family you can stay with for a while. When you lose your ability to gain financial capital, you lean on the relational capital you've built up.

This is essentially what the rich man's manager was doing in Jesus' parable in Luke 16. He knew he was about to be fired (losing his financial capital), so he said, "I know what I'll do so that when I lose my job here, people will welcome me into their houses." He then used the financial capital still at his disposal to "buy friends" (grow his relational capital) so he would have a place to stay when he lost his job. It's fascinating that Jesus explicitly says to do this at the end of the parable: "Use worldly wealth to gain friends for yourselves." It's a wise investment!

Relational capital *is* more valuable than physical, intellectual and financial capital because you really can't do anything of value in life without a relationship with others, in which there is at least some level of mutual trust. In essence, you can't really *do* anything with your physical, intellectual or financial capital unless you have at least a little relational capital.

In the Gospels, we see Jesus consistently invest in relational capital and train his disciples to do the same. Once he chose twelve of his disciples to be designated apostles, he prioritized his time and investment in those individuals, developing deep relational capital with them as he trained them. We also see him repeatedly returning to the home of Mary, Martha and Lazarus in Bethany, cultivating relational capital with them and using their home as a base of operations as well as a place of retreat.

Jesus grew his relational capital by investing his physical capital in his covenant relationships. The covenant relationship Jesus forged with his disciples formed the basis of the kingdom breakthrough he was able to achieve through them.

Interestingly, it appears that investing relationally in this way was one of the ways Jesus paid his bills. At one point, Jesus is traveling from village to village with his 12 disciples, "... and also some women who had been cured of evil spirits and diseases. These women were helping to support them out of their own means."[28] Jesus invested relational capital and received financial capital.

Physical Capital

Physical capital is how much *time and energy* we have to invest. The currency of physical capital is *hours and health*.

As we descend our hierarchy of capital, *physical capital* is next. This refers to our ability to devote time and energy to people and projects. It includes the time we make available, as well as the capacity we have to use that time. Our overall health comes into play here, because it greatly affects our ability to invest our time and energy.

One key way we can invest in physical capital is by simply honoring the limitations we have as humans. Getting proper rest and living in a rhythm of life that allows us to work hard *and* play hard is essential if we are going to steward our long-term physical capital. This capital is also the great equalizer. We all have the same 24 hours, in a way—it's a matter of using the higher capitals to discern what to do with our limited time here on earth.

Jesus shows us how to do this. Obviously Jesus had a body, which was his "power pack" of physical capital that allowed him to heal, preach and train his disciples. He did not bypass the normal disciplines that need to accompany being human. He slept at night most of the time, walked from place to place, used language to communicate ideas, touched people as he healed them and sat down and ate regular meals with others. He got tired when he did all those things, so he sometimes needed to take a nap. This is normal human stuff.

Jesus constantly stewarded his physical capital and trained his disciples to do the same. After Jesus sent his disciples out on their first short missionary journey, things started to get busy. "Then, because so many people were coming and going, they did not even have a chance to eat, he said to them, 'Come with me by yourselves to a quiet place and get some rest.'"[29]

Jesus taught his disciples that there are seasons of bearing fruit and seasons of "abiding," when the fruit is pruned back and we spend a season *not* visibly bearing fruit.[30] Like a vine branch that has been pruned, we simply abide in the vine for a season, receiving nourishment from the vine while nothing is visibly happening on the outside. Jesus demonstrated that we need to embrace the pruning seasons or we won't bear fruit.

WHETHER YOU CALL IT A MENTAL HEALTH DAY OR JUST PLAIN-OLD VACATION, THE RESULTS ARE IN—INVESTING IN OUR PHYSICAL CAPITAL PAYS HUGE DIVIDENDS IN THE LONG RUN.

These instructions mirrored God's design in creation, where he rested on the "seventh day," creating a model for humanity to take one day out a week to set our work aside and rest. This might not seem like a big deal, but when God wanted to tell his people the top ten things to remember about what it means to be his people, taking a day off came in at number four! "Remember the Sabbath day by keeping it holy."[31]

Many business leaders today recognize this. At least every month a new article or podcast promotes the benefits of taking proper time off from work, and how productivity actually *increases* when employees stop working long hours. Just do an Internet search for "benefits of taking a day off," and you'll find dozens of resources. Whether you call it a mental health day or just plain-old vacation, the results are in—investing in our physical capital pays huge dividends in the long run.

Jesus, of course, knew this (brilliant economist that he was!) Physical capital is quite valuable, and worth stewarding well. Investing in our ability to spend time on people and projects shouldn't be taken for granted. It needs to be invested in intentionally.

Likewise, Paul encouraged the Ephesians to invest their physical and intellectual capital wisely when he wrote, "Be very careful, then, how you live—not as unwise but as wise, making the most of every opportunity, because the days are evil. Therefore do not be foolish, but understand what the Lord's will is."[32]

As a side note, some people wonder whether physical capital should really be ranked higher than intellectual capital and financial capital. Think about it this way: If you're sick, you can't work (financial capital). Likewise, if you have a migraine, you can't deliver a lecture or read a book (intellectual capital). You can't solve a problem in a brainstorming meeting if you're in the hospital because of a heart attack. No amount of money or ideas can replace the value of being physically present, giving time and attention to people or projects. The health of our bodies, which translates into our ability to invest time and energy, is of significant value.

Intellectual Capital

Intellectual capital is the amount of *creativity, ideas and knowledge* we have to invest. The currency of intellectual capital is *insights and ideas*; information and application.

Moving down on the hierarchy is *intellectual capital*, which refers to the knowledge we've acquired, as well as our ability to bring ideas and creative solutions to the table. This is of higher value than financial capital because we can't create ideas and be creative simply by spending a lot of money. Intellectual capital comes from something deeper than what money can buy. We can throw all the money in the world at a problem, but it won't get solved until someone brings some intellectual capital to bear, coming up with a creative and workable solution.

Jesus possessed an astonishing level of intellectual capital, which he used often in his mission. In the culture of his day, Jesus was recognized by the crowds, his disciples and even his enemies as a rabbi, which means "teacher" or "master." A rabbi was a teacher of the Jewish law, someone who had studied very rigorously; someone who knew what he was talking about. In fact, after Jesus was resurrected, the first word out of the mouth of the first person to see Jesus alive was, "Rabboni!" (a form of rabbi).

Jesus wasn't just a holy person who prayed a lot—he was also a smart person who thought a lot. He had intellectual capital, and he used it to train his disciples, teach the crowds and answer his critics. After a little talk he did on a hillside (traditionally called the Sermon on the Mount), the Bible says, "... the crowds were amazed at his teaching, because he taught as one who had authority, and not as their teachers of the law."[33]

When the Pharisees (a religious sect within Judaism) tried to trap Jesus by asking him a tricky and politically loaded question about paying the imperial tax to Caesar, he answered in an astonishingly clever and prophetic way.

> Finding the coin used to pay the tax, Jesus asked them, "Whose image is this? And whose inscription?"
>
> "Caesar's," they replied.
>
> So Jesus answered them, "So give back to Caesar what is Caesar's, and to God what is God's."
>
> The Bible simply says, "When they heard this, they were amazed. So they left him and went away."[34]
>
> That same day the Sadducees (another religious sect) tried to trap Jesus with an obtuse question about marriage laws. He answered them with such clarity and biblical insight that when the crowds heard it they were "astonished at his teaching."[35]

In addition to answering the Jewish questioners and amazing the crowds, Jesus primarily used his intellectual capital to train his disciples. He was constantly explaining his parables to the disciples, teaching them to understand the kingdom of God at a very deep level.

In short, Jesus was no slouch when it came to intelligence and creativity. He used many metaphors and parables to help people grasp the amazing mysteries of God.

The same challenge is here for us—we need to be life-learners of knowledge, always seeking to grab ahold of the wisdom in front of us and quickly release it to those around us, just like Jesus did.

Financial Capital

Financial capital is how much *treasure* we have to invest. The currency of financial capital is, of course, money: *dollars and cents*; pounds and pennies, etc.

Although it ranks lowest in our hierarchy, we are most familiar with this capital because we work with it every day. Financial capital is simply the money we have available to invest. Although this is easy to understand conceptually, we can easily get into trouble in the way that we relate to it, a problem that typically happens in one of two ways.

The first way we get into trouble is by overvaluing financial capital. Society in our day (just as in Jesus' day) often values financial capital as life's most important thing. We sacrifice all kinds of other capital to get it, even though it never quite fulfills its promises to us. Countless stories, books and movies share the storyline of risking everything for the big financial payoff.

In fact, studies have shown that, after a certain threshold of income is reached, obtaining more money has almost no effect on our overall happiness or quality of life.[36] As soon as we have enough, getting more money doesn't really seem to create greater life satisfaction. Yet we continue to behave as if it will.

Jesus reminds us that financial capital is only one form of capital, and that if we can cash it all in to "buy shares" in a more valuable form of capital, we are wise!

Jesus also said, "It is more blessed to give than to receive,"[37] and in fact, even secular studies support this notion. Michael Norton, as associate professor at Harvard Business School, conducted a survey, the results of which indicate that when money is invested *in others* instead of ourselves, it actually increases our happiness.[38] It turns out money *can* buy happiness—we just need to invest it in the right place.

The second way we get into trouble is by devaluing financial capital entirely, looking at it as somehow evil or tainted. Since overvaluation is a problem on one end of the spectrum, we figure that devaluing money entirely must be the virtue on the opposite side. Many people take pride in the fact that they "don't care about money," and have very little of it.

Not having money doesn't make us happy, as anyone who has lived in poverty knows. Being poor doesn't automatically make anyone virtuous. Likewise, having a lot of money doesn't make someone evil. A lack of financial capital is a lack, a limitation. Many people who take pride in having very little money are dependent on those who have some to spare.

It's important to acknowledge that there is nothing inherently wrong with having money, even with having a lot of it. Many of the patriarchs in the Old Testament (Abraham, Isaac, Joseph, etc.) were very wealthy people. Nowhere in the Bible does it say that money is evil. The *love* of money is a massive problem, of course (which is the overvaluing problem). But we needn't throw out the baby (financial capital) with the bathwater (the love of money). Living hand-to-mouth isn't holier than being wealthy.

Growing Your Spiritual Capital

Recently my friend sent me an article from *Business Insider* on a man named Markus Persson. The headline read, "I've never felt more isolated: The man who sold Minecraft to Microsoft for $2.5 billion reveals the empty side of success." For those of you who (like me) don't know the video game culture, Markus Persson is a Swedish video game programmer and designer who reportedly has a net worth of $1.5 billion. That's billion with a b.

In one of his more authentic tweets he shared, "Hanging out in Ibiza with a bunch of friends and partying with famous people, able to do whatever I want, and I've never felt more isolated."

Unfortunately, like Markus we often learn the importance of the order of the capitals the hard way. We pursue financial and intellectual capital with everything God has put into us and end up feeling emptier than when we started. My guess is you can even think of someone who is currently struggling and whose solution (more than likely) could be found in prioritizing the order of his or her capitals.

The key for them and for all of us is the same: we must prioritize the right capitals in the right order. It's how we seek first the kingdom, and trust that the rest of the capitals will be taken care of.

Luke 6:49 says, "But the one who hears my words and does not put them into practice is like a man who built a house on the ground without a foundation. The moment the torrent struck that house, it collapsed and its destruction was complete."

Now that we have heard and understood God's kingdom business, it's in our best interest to put these words into practice, building a foundation that won't collapse in the storm.

Let's look back to the parable of the wise and the foolish builder to help drive this point home. Jesus said,

> "Therefore everyone who hears these words of mine and puts them into practice is like a wise man who built his house on the rock. The rain came down, the streams rose, and the winds blew and beat against that house; yet it did not fall, because it had its foundation on the rock. But everyone who hears these words of mine and does not put them into practice is like a foolish man who built his house on sand. The rain came down, the streams rose, and the winds blew and beat against that house, and it fell with a great crash."
> — Matthew 7:24-27

Here again we find Jesus using the language of the builder, and the interesting thing is that both builders in the story *heard* the words of Jesus. Perhaps they agreed with the words or even felt inspired by them. The only difference was that one of the builders *put them into practice*, and this made all the difference.

Putting Jesus' words into practice makes us like a wise builder. Hearing Jesus' words but doing nothing about them makes us like a foolish builder. *Putting Jesus' words into practice is how we grow our spiritual capital.*

So as we walk through life, read the Scripture and spend our time at work, rest and play, we are continually asking:
1. What is God saying to me?
2. What am I going to do about it?[39]

These two simple questions will keep us asking for his wisdom, in order that we can grow our spiritual capital.

I definitely don't always get this order right, so I continue to work to make spiritual capital (life with Jesus) my main priority. Yet wisdom and knowledge are power, and so the more I understand God's kingdom business, the more wisdom and power flow from my life and into the lives of others.

Ultimately, isn't this the goal of his kingdom?

So what connects all the capitals? What's the foundational reality that flows through them all? It's love. That's right—love. "For God so loved the world, that he gave his one and only son that whomever should believe in him will not perish but have eternal life."[40] It's because of God's love that spiritual capital on this earth is even possible.

And so … "Love the Lord your God with all your heart and with all your soul and with all your mind. This is the first and greatest commandment. And the second is like it: love your neighbor as yourself. All the Law and the Prophets hang on these two commandments."[41]

How else can I impact my family, friends, co-workers and community if I am not first prioritizing spiritual capital with everything he has invested in me?

It's a priority, a process and a plan that I am building into my life each and every day.

One that yields an abundant return.

Discussion Questions

1. Do you value capital in the same way Jesus does? Where are there differences? Have you ever made a decision to choose some other form of capital above spiritual capital? What were the results?

2. If an objective observer looked at the way you spend your time and was asked to put the five forms of capital in value order for your life, what would that order be?

3. What would it look like for you to rearrange the way you value the five forms of capital so they line up with the way Jesus says they are to be prioritized?

4. Have you ever thought about your relationships with family and friends as a form of capital that can grow or decline? What are the implications of seeing our relationship with God as a form of capital that we can invest in?

5. How can you practically start putting these principles into practice today?

Putting It Into Practice

Matt & Betsy Wilhelm,
American Heart Association, Regional Manager / Stay-at-Home Mom

As we look back over our journey of implementing the Five Capitals in our life, our most transformational decision was to truly pursue spiritual capital. Through studying the words, works and ways of Jesus, we realized God was calling us to more intimacy and connection with him. As we've opened more of our lives to him, we've naturally seen more order and fruit in the four other capitals. We have cultivated and engaged in relationships with a mind and a heart to love like Jesus loves. God is slowly teaching us how to love others, even when that love isn't reciprocated, appreciated or noticed. We have become less selfish in our love of the people around us.

Also, we are more honorable with our time and our home. We use our time to bless others as we try to be where we say we will be and do what we say we will do. We've opened our home to family, friends and even strangers as the Lord has led people into our lives. Our pursuit of intellectual capital is being refined as well. We are pursuing knowledge that is a blessing to the kingdom and a blessing to those around us. We are using our time to wisely invest in intellectual capital. Learning about things that we feel God is showing us will bless people and advance his kingdom.

Lastly, we see God removing a poverty mentality from us when it comes to money. We are beginning to view financial resources in a different light. We are no longer holding on so tightly to money and possessions, and instead seeing these as tools to bless and love on people around us. While there is still much for us to learn on this journey, it is amazing to see how much the Lord has changed our hearts. And for us, the order of the Five Capitals all began to shift when we made the decision to pursue spiritual capital. It has been an amazing and life-changing experience; one we pray all will enter into.

Chapter Five
PERSISTENCE:
INTEGRATING YOUR LIFE

The key is not to prioritize what's on your schedule
but to schedule your priorities.
— Stephen Covey

I have fought the good fight, I have finished the race, I have kept the faith.
— 2 Timothy 4:7

Keeping Things in Order

It started with a long look in the mirror. I was fat. The doctor had confirmed it just hours before. "If you keep on this path, given your medical history, you'll be due for a heart attack within the next 10 to 15 years." I was 25. The lack of exercise, corporate dinners, bad eating habits and four years of continuous weight gain in college had caught up with me. Something had to change. My priorities were all out of order. I had been investing in the wrong things. Putting financial capital on top and using intellectual and relational capital to get there meant spiritual and physical capital were decidedly at the bottom.

I was so focused on the next promotion that the long hours at work left little time for exercise or consistent eating. So I regrouped and made some changes. I got up early because the workout never happened after work, and I had to stop kidding myself. I found an exercise and eating plan (thanks Body for Life!) and found a workout partner. Ironically this was my brother Matt, who had just moved his family to Indianapolis to work with the same company I worked for. In just 10 months, and 62 pounds later, my clothes fit and my priorities changed. Investing in one capital had helped the other capitals, and life improved.

God wants us to flourish in all five capitals, not just one or two. A well-lived life means whole life abundance. As we saw in my story and that of the lottery winner William Post's life, we also need to pay close attention to the *order* of the five capitals.

The five capitals are set up in a hierarchy that identifies their relative value, and it's very important to keep things *in that order*, investing as though the most important things are actually the most important. For example, if we have an opportunity to invest some of our financial and physical capital to grow our spiritual capital (paying a spiritual director or coach, for example), this should be a no-brainer. We are investing a lower-value capital (financial) to grow a higher-value capital (spiritual).

Yet it's somewhat difficult to keep these things in proper perspective. Most of us don't automatically make financial investments to grow our spiritual capital, because we probably overvalue financial capital.

Often the problem is that we tend to build our investment strategies on "quick returns" rather than patiently waiting for more valuable investments to mature over time. Financial capital gives us the quickest return, and so we tend to focus our investment strategies there. All the capitals above financial take longer to grow, but they are also more valuable and last longer. Spiritual capital, the most valuable capital, lasts *forever*.

Another reason it's difficult for us to keep our capitals in their proper place is that the institutions and cultures of our day (just as the ones in Jesus' day) tend to put the five capitals in a different order, and relentlessly train us to think similarly. There are quite a few competing value systems out there.

The World of Business

For example, let's think about the business world, where financial capital is valued the highest. The profit motive specifically points to *financial* profit. Everything else is leveraged to grow financial capital. Acquiring more money is seen as the point of business. So the business world might list the five capitals in the following order of value:

1. Financial: It's all about the bottom line.
2. Intellectual: The most competent get promoted.
3. Relational: Engage with people to grow your business.
4. Physical: Go without sleep or exercise, if that's what it takes.
5. Spiritual: You're welcome to worship whomever you'd like.

After the ultimate goal of making money (financial capital), ideas and creativity (intellectual capital) are the next highest capital because they can be leveraged to make more money. After that comes relational capital, since business happens only where relationships are strong. Physical capital is near the bottom, because it's generally acceptable to sacrifice your health to work more hours, and last on the list is spiritual capital, because it's rarely even considered to have any value.

If we've been influenced by the business world, no wonder it's difficult to keep our concerns about financial capital in check. We have been trained to think it is the most important capital, when it is, in fact, the *least* important.

Eventually, life stops working properly, because we've made a foolish investment, sacrificing capital that was in fact more valuable (spiritual, relational, physical) to grow capital that was less valuable (financial).

Here's another way this plays out: moving halfway across the country to take a great job opportunity is regarded as wise and sensible, although moving halfway across the country to join a great community would be regarded as foolish and even a little weird.

So if we have our capitals in order, we ought to prioritize the who question before the *what* question.

Who are the members of the family we are called to be on mission with?

Once God has highlighted them to us, we must invest our capital to be part of that family and trust that the relational capital we build will eventually translate into financial capital we can live on. The fact that this paragraph puzzles us testifies to how backward we have this priority.

At least once a month someone in my family hollers, "Let's go to Chick-fil-A." Then immediately, this desire is followed by groans as we all remember it's Sunday and Chick-fil-A is closed. Maybe you have experienced that scenario as well?

Regardless of momentary disappointment, this is a great example of how a company has prioritized spiritual capital above all the other capitals, and the irony here is that other great companies like Google and Apple actually prioritize the capitals in the correct order.

The Prioritized Business
1. Spiritual: It's about our brand identity, living out the company's Vision and Values.
2. Relational: People are our biggest asset, so we create a healthy, productive culture.
3. Physical: We know the rhythms of our business and take a marathon mentality.
4. Intellectual: We hire well, develop and train our people, and promote from within.
5. Financial: We steward our resources, invest wisely, and grow our market share.

The World of Academia

Let's think about the academic world. The capital of highest value is *intellectual*. Accumulating and passing on knowledge are seen as the highest good in the academic environment. If you are a professor, it's generally about how many books you're written, the papers you're publishing and what letters are behind your name. Perhaps the full order of capitals goes something like this:
1. Intellectual: Knowledge and innovation is key, as you have to be on the cutting-edge of insight and ideas.
2. Financial: Money makes the world go around. The bigger the endowment, the more the university can do.
3. Relational: We need more students to grow, as well as engaged alumni to give.
4. Physical: Our campus must be beautiful. Students want to inhabit the best housing and recreation facilities.

5. Spiritual: Unless you're a faith-based organization, this capital is at the bottom. You're welcome to worship whomever you'd like.

Where do we see this high value on finances and intellect? One just has to look at the ever increasing tuition rates or the ACT/SAT standards of admission at our nation's top schools to see the value and the priority. The world of academia admits the sharpest students and hires the best professors. This brings in the most money and creates a loyal alumni base, allowing for beautiful campus buildings and apartment-style living, which attracts the smartest students, and so on. The life you get when you invest in this order is a different kind of life from the one you get when you invest in the business-world order. Spending vast amounts of money to get a Ph.D. is seen as a worthy investment, because intellectual capital is valued more highly than financial capital. But spiritual capital is again at the bottom, as Jesus is not taken seriously in the secular academic world as someone who has *knowledge* about life.

The Entertainment World

Moving along, let's focus on a few areas we all know and love—movies, sports and all things entertaining. With celebrities taking center stage, I am tempted to say this could be the most influential area and thus the ordering of capitals we fall most prey to. Our TV commercials, magazines and social media are flooded with images, videos and posts that pertain to our physical appearance. There's a continual market in our society to look, feel and be perfect in every way.

In regards to sports, thanks to athletes' amazing physical abilities, we repeatedly elevate winning teams and individuals. They are kings and queens in our culture. It's all too easy to put them on a pedestal when they achieve incredible success.

When I lived in Kentucky in 2012, the Kentucky Wildcat basketball team had an incredible year and defeated Kansas for the national championship. It wasn't hard for me to become a believer in Coach John Calipari, make plans around the games and buy more Kentucky gear. (I'm still a huge fan today—Go Cats!)

Something about entertainment—whether it's sports, movies or otherwise—puts us in awe, grabs our attention and reorients our life around the value society places on each of these capitals. If I were to guess the order of capitals in this world, I think this is how it would go.

1. Physical: Performance and/or appearance rule.
2. Financial: Who has and makes the most money is at the top.
3. Relational: The more fans we have, the more money we make.
4. Intellectual: Great directors produce blockbusters and great coaches produce winning teams.
5. Spiritual: It's better to be politically correct, unless you're Tim Tebow.

The Church World

Now I wish we could say the church gets it right, but they are also susceptible to living out less-than-ideal order. How do most churches value the Five Capitals? How does yours? The order is easiest to determine by looking at a church's *measurements of success*. What do we leverage all our capital for? I find that most churches are primarily about two things: attendance and giving. How many were there on Sunday, and what was the weekly offering amount? They measure physical capital and financial capital.

In many churches, the full order looks something like this:

1. Physical: How many people are at church on Sunday?
2. Financial: Is every member tithing each month?
3. Relational: Is the Body of Christ meeting in community?
4. Spiritual: Are people engaging with Jesus each week?
5. Intellectual: Are the members growing in their walk with God?

Of course every tradition is a bit different. Our more historic churches are often heavily influenced by the academic world, leading them to place a high value on intellectual capital. Many Southern Baptist churches, for example, emphasize the "right parsing of the Word," focusing on the right meaning (or interpretation) of Scripture. Recently there's been a trend within many evangelical, non-denominational churches toward elevating relational capital, promoting an "anyone and everyone is welcome" environment. If these churches aren't careful, this can become more about the right exegesis or people engagement rather than a relationship with God.

Even our church culture must be diligent and pro-active in putting our five capitals in the right order. Because any wrong order always leads to foolish investments and a life that just doesn't work.

> **BECAUSE ANY WRONG ORDER ALWAYS LEADS TO FOOLISH INVESTMENTS AND A LIFE THAT JUST DOESN'T WORK**

Temperament

Even the way we are wired can create challenges in keeping the capitals in order. Take the Myers-Briggs personality assessment, for example. "Thinkers" tend to put intellectual capital toward the top, while "feelers" tend to put relational capital on top.[42]

Family

Reflecting on these competing cultural systems, it's no wonder children struggle. School says to live life one way, ESPN another and their youth pastor another. That's a lot for a child to sort through. Yet the priorities can be set in the home—the place where kids (hopefully) spend most of their time. How are the Five Capitals prioritized in your family? What about in the family you grew up in? What kinds of capitals are invested in consistently?

Are you the academic family—the family that values intellectual capital above everything else? Would your kids rather sacrifice a good night's sleep to get an A on that test or go to bed on time and settle for a B? How would you feel about their decision?

Maybe you're the athletic family that places physical capital at the top of the list. How much family relational time is sacrificed so the kids can participate in sports? It's not wrong to play team sports, of course, just like it isn't wrong to get an A on a test. But it's worth asking the question: Which capitals are at the top of your family's list?

Perhaps the family culture values mom's career or dad's career above everything else. Advancement and promotion are the highest good to be sought, and other capitals are invested to ensure the growth of financial capital.

Here's a breakdown of where the emphasis lies when each capital is on top.

SPIRITUAL		
▶*Wise Family*	▶*Honored by all*	▶*Contagious & Compelling*
RELATIONAL		
▶*Adored Family*	▶*Loved by all*	▶*Kind & Sweet*
PHYSICAL		
▶*Gorgeous Family*	▶*Envied by all*	▶*Competitive & Strong*
INTELLECTUAL		
▶*Smartest Family*	▶*Know it all*	▶*Smart & Sharp*
FINANCIAL		
▶*Richest Family*	▶*Have it all*	▶*Wealthy & Prestigious*

How we order the capitals in our personal life will naturally overflow to our family, which is why it's so crucial to make sure we are following God's order. The last thing we want to communicate to our family and friends is a life with the capitals in the wrong order.

Recognizing Capital

Let's use a biblical example: Acts 6 tells a story about investment and capital in the economy of the early church. The number of disciples was increasing, and a very normal thing happened—conflict. The Hellenistic Jews complained against the Hebraic Jews because they felt their widows were being overlooked in the distribution of food. (It's remarkable to think about how sophisticated a system of food distribution they must have had for this to even become an issue!)

The 12 apostles gathered to try to decide what to do. Their decision:

> It would not be right for us to neglect the ministry of the word of God in order to wait on tables. Brothers and sisters, choose seven men from among you who are known to be full of the Spirit and wisdom. We will turn this responsibility over to them and will give our attention to prayer and the ministry of the word. — Acts 6:2

"This proposal pleased the whole group," the text says, so that's what they did. I've heard some commentators suspect that this wasn't actually the right decision on behalf of the apostles, that somehow they were trying to get out of the menial task of waiting on tables and making sure everyone got their fair share of food.

If we look at it through the lens of the Five Capitals, we see that they weren't trying to avoid serving. They were simply recognizing that the best way for them to serve was not by waiting on tables, but by attending to prayer and the ministry of the Word. They recognized that they were investing so much physical capital in the food distribution that they weren't able to invest their spiritual capital in the community.

There were lots of godly people who could wait on tables, but the apostles were the only ones in the community who had spent three years with Jesus. Physical capital is valuable and necessary, but spiritual capital is *more* valuable, and the apostles had an abundance of spiritual capital to invest in the community. Freeing them up ended up being the greatest investment decision for the entire group.

You can see from these examples how practically helpful this framework can be when it comes to finding the abundant life Jesus wants to give us—it doesn't only bless us, but everyone around us as well. We get a return on our investment, and so do others! This is actually the point. When our capital grows, we aren't the only ones who benefit—our friends and family benefit as well, because we share our additional capital with others (which is actually *investing* it, after all).

Imagine a whole community doing this together—investing its capital in each other, seeing it grow and grow.

Growing Your Capital

I can hear some of you muttering now: "Great, I get the order," you say, "but how do I grow capital in the areas that are deficient?"

To grow one of the Five Capitals, you invest the other four.

When I first became a Christian, I went to bed earlier, partied less and went to church and Bible study. I was using my physical capital to invest in my newfound spiritual capital. In addition, I was reading the Bible, engaging in spiritual conversation and meeting new friends who also loved Jesus—growing both my relational capital and my intellectual capital. Lastly, I used my money to buy books and CDs, which used my financial capital to once again invest in my spiritual capital.

Without even knowing it at that time, I was using all the other four capitals to invest in the most valuable capital. This same process is equally effective with every capital.

Remember my story of losing weight? You might be wondering how, exactly, I lost all that weight. I simply invested the other four capitals in the one that was deficient:

Spiritual: I prayed for God's grace and strength to get up in the morning, eat well and stop going to comfort food to relax.

Relational: I realized it was easier to get to the gym with friends, and I asked for accountability and support.

Physical: I used the other capitals to focus on improving my physical health.

Intellectual: I read books, blogs and articles on ways to improve my health and stay in shape.

Financial: I invested in a gym membership and purchased better food options.

As you can see, it's still important to keep the order in order. Just because God highlights a specific area to you doesn't mean it should take first priority over your life. He is still your No. 1 pursuit, and consequently you will have greater success in the area you want to improve by keeping him as your top priority.

Discussion Questions

1. On your worst day, what's the order of your capitals? What is the hardest part for you in keeping your desired order of the capitals?

2. What was the order of the capitals for you when you were growing up?

3. When you read through the descriptions of the various orders in the business, sports, temperament worlds, etc., which one do you most relate to and connect with?

4. As you reflect on your family life, what do you discern is the current order of each of the capitals? What is one way you can start to re-emphasize the correct order within your family?

5. When you observe your professional work environment, what do you think is the order of the capitals? How can you be an influence who encourages the correct order?

6. Is God currently highlighting a specific capital to you? If so, how can you use the other four capitals to invest in the highlighted one?

Putting It Into Practice

Craig Cheney, Trainer, Coach, Pastor at Heartland Community Church
For most, myself included, we spend our years accumulating a conglomeration of ideas, experiences, models and practices, which we hope will produce the abundant life God promises us. The typical "fruit" of this approach is not fullness of life but loss of life ... lost years, lost fulfillment, lost relationships, lost resources and lost hope.

Instead of loss, I have found abiding hope and genuine gain as I've oriented my life perspective, priorities and practices around those of Jesus and his framework for life. When I'm most focused on growing my spiritual capital, I experience the greatest peace, fulfillment and fruitfulness in every other aspect of my life. When I get it upside down and focus on my financial or intellectual capital as my primary means of peace, fulfillment and fruitfulness, I grow anxious, fearful, insecure and unfulfilled.

While the operating system around me declares that financial, intellectual and physical capital provides the fullest life, my experience has been the opposite. The matters closest to my heart are given life, vitality and fullness when I honor the priorities, patterns and practices of Jesus in his life-giving framework. When I finish and start my day focused on hearing from God, I find I'm able to hear his voice throughout my day. When I intentionally orient myself to grow my relational capital, I find it brings community, order, freshness and joy to every other endeavor. Jesus' framework and "asset" priorities for the way life works are taking root in me and the way I live my life. As I embrace it, integrate it and offer it to others, the fulfillment of life is multiplied.

CHAPTER SIX
POWER:
MAKING A DIFFERENCE

Never doubt that a small group of thoughtful committed citizens
can change the world; indeed, it's the only thing that ever has.
— Margaret Mead

The Father and I are one.
— John 10:30

The Rocketeer

Growing up in nowhere Iowa, one of the things I enjoyed most was going to the movies. But at age 11, the movies my parents allowed me to see were mostly in the vein of *Ernest Goes to Camp* (1987) and *The Little Mermaid* (1989). I was dying to see all the great action films my older brother had been to, movies like *Star Wars*, *Indiana Jones* and *The Goonies*.

You can imagine my delight when, after a long day at the Franklin County Fair, a good friend of mine named Austin invited me to see the premiere of *The Rocketeer*. Of course I wanted to go see it, as the TV commercials had hyped this as the greatest action movie of all time.

Our local theatre was old-school awesome as well, not like the small-screen, boxy rooms of today. The screen was of IMAX proportions, the floor was slanted and there was a full balcony complete with a soft drink and popcorn for just $1. Can you believe my parents said yes? I loved every minute.

If you happened to miss this 1991 summer blockbuster, the story line is essentially this: a stunt pilot, in love with a girl, finds a personal rocket backpack, which the

Nazis are developing to conquer the world. After lots of action, twists and turns, the hero saves the day and gets the girl.

I know, I know, why can't they make movies with plots like this anymore?

What did this movie do for me? It planted a seed that said, **"You can achieve the American Dream. You can grow up, be the hero, get the girl and have everything in life."** Until I found God in college, that's exactly what I went after.

As I've gotten older (and a little wiser), I've realized that while many think this way, it isn't actually true. It's not even true in the movies. Sure, the superhero gets all the fame and glory, but he's only there because of the team of supporters, teammates and fellow heroes around him (or her). How quickly this essential supporting cast is forgotten! In reality, when these superheroes are alone is when they're the most vulnerable and susceptible to failure. Consider these examples:

Would Iron Man have made it without his assistant Pepper Potts? Would Batman have survived without Robin? Or Butler Alfred? Or even Cat Woman? Can you imagine Starsky without Hutch? Thelma without Louise? The great teams and duos go on and on. Bonnie and Clyde. Superman and Lois Lane. The Avengers. The X-Men. The Fellowship of the Ring. Frodo has Sam. Bond has M (and Q). Minnie has Mickey—and Donald, Daisy, Goofy and Pluto. Sherlock? Watson.

The music industry and the sports world are the same. Imagine Sonny without Cher. There are power couples: Beyonce and Jay-Z. Brangelina, Will Smith and Jada Pinkett. Magicians Penn and Teller. The great Rodgers and Hammerstein. Simon and Garfunkel. Jordan and Pippen. Shaq and Kobe. Montana and Rice.

I rest my case.

Every great hero has a counterpart, a helper—*a team.*

The Bible is no different. We see that those who won great victories *never did it alone*. They were always supported by a friend or joined by a team. Ruth stayed with Naomi. Adam and Eve. Jonathan saved David. Noah and his sons.

David's military victories came with his Mighty Men, the chief three and the 33.[43] Moses led God's people out of Egypt, across the Red Sea and through the desert for 40 years. By his side the whole time were his brother and sister, Aaron and Miriam, and his understudy Joshua. Paul did ministry alongside lots of people—Luke, Timothy, Barnabas, Priscilla, Philemon, Epaphras and more.

As the saying goes, you can't have one without the other!

Left alone, each of these individuals would never have been able to make it, let alone fulfill his or her full potential. Obviously some of these superhero characters are fictional, but the truth remains—two is better than one, and if you are in a battle (and we *are* in a battle) you want an army on your side. If we're going to accomplish all that God has for us, we want comrades around us. Yes, we need those closest to us, a wider support group and the whole body working together if we are going to maximize our impact here on this earth.

Life and leadership don't have to be lonely, and they shouldn't be lonely. *It's not supposed to be lonely.* Many of us over-work alone and burn out. If we ever do arrive, we do so largely isolated with no one with whom to share the blessings. There has to be a better way of leading and living that's fuller and more fun.

So let's look at Jesus. If anyone could do it on his own, it was him. He was perfect! But when we look at his life, we see that he had not only one, but two teams. Jesus came to earth as part of a spiritual team with the Father and the Holy Spirit. He prayed and talked to his Father daily, saying things like:

"I only do what I see the Father and I doing."[44]

"The Father and I are one."[45]

"Father, may they be one like You and I are one.[46]

> ## LIFE AND LEADERSHIP DON'T HAVE TO BE LONELY, AND THEY SHOULDN'T BE LONELY. *IT'S NOT SUPPOSED TO BE LONELY.*

> **SIMPLY PUT, INDIVIDUALISM ISN'T IN GOD'S VOCABULARY.**

He walked and worked in the power of the Holy Spirit daily. He was never alone.

In fact, we see that community was such a non-negotiable that, when he was initially rejected by his biological family, he immediately found followers who started as friends and eventually functioned as family. He called them his disciples, and from that moment on he had three (Peter, James and John), 12 (his disciples) and the 72 (whom he sent out). After that initial rejection by his family (who eventually came around), it would have been easy to say, "Forget it—I can do this by myself." Yet his story truly is a communal one.

In fact, it's all communal. Jesus came with his heavenly family to rescue and reconcile his orphaned family, to connect us back to the family so we might go and bring others into the family as one, the Body of Christ. Simply put, *individualism isn't in God's vocabulary.*

However, it's most certainly in ours. Let's briefly reflect on the few sources of our current love affair with individualism. Our American forefathers established the rights of the individual (a.k.a. the Bill of Rights) and in some ways justifiably so given the abuse and oppression of the European ruling class. Secular philosophy has also helped to promote individualism, with philosophers like Rene Descartes being quoted saying, "I think, therefore I am," helping to plant the seed and grow the idea of me, myself and I.

The irony is we intuitively know this way of individualistic thinking isn't true or right. None of us can survive on our own. We need each other.

A Biblical Framework

Are you living in isolation? Are you ready to find your team? Do you know others who need you on their team?

Maybe a better question is: How do we find our team? What exactly should we be looking for? In Genesis 2 we find some answers.

> Then the LORD God formed the man from the dust of the ground. He breathed the breath of life into the man's nostrils, and the man became a living person.
>
> Then the LORD God planted a garden in Eden in the east, and there he placed the man he had made. The LORD God made all sorts of trees grow up from the ground—trees that were beautiful and that produced delicious fruit. In the middle of the garden he placed the tree of life and the tree of the knowledge of good and evil.
>
> The LORD God placed the man in the Garden of Eden to tend and watch over it. But the LORD God warned him, "You may freely eat the fruit of every tree in the garden—except the tree of the knowledge of good and evil. If you eat its fruit, you are sure to die."
>
> Then the LORD God said, "It is not good for the man to be alone."
> — Genesis 2:7-17

What? Not good for man to be alone? Here Adam is perfect. There's no feeling guilty about getting home late. No fights with his wife. All his ideas can be good ones. The TV remote is all his. And not to mention he's perfectly connected to God the Father who happens to be King of the universe and is providing for all his needs. What's the problem here?

Even in a perfect state of being, it was not good for Adam to be alone. He needed to be in relationship—not just with God, but with others. Being created in the image of God, one essential relationship was missing. He needed community, a co-laborer, a helper. He needed a teammate.

Two specific realities seem to be in play here.
1. He's incomplete: There was a real *desire for more*.
2. He needs help: The work can't get done *on his own*.

> **FINDING OUR *EZER KENEGDOS* IN LIFE IS A KEY COMPONENT TO DISCOVERING LIFE TO THE FULL.**

Notice God gave him the directive to work—yet nothing happens until after Eve is created.

God had the solution. "I will make a helper suitable for him."

The original Hebrew words translated here are *ezer kenegdo*. Their definitions are:

> *ezer* = ideal or perfect helper
> *kenegdo* = suitable, complimentary companion

Both words are essential. *Ezer* is the work or kingdom component—a co-laborer to get things done. *Kenegdo* is the relational piece—a companion for community, covenant and connection. Most people focus too much on the *what* and not enough on the *who* they are called to do life with. Finding our ezer kenegdos in life is a key component to discovering life to the full.

Adam connected with Eve, and away they went. David befriended Jonathan, who saved his life, Ruth stuck with Naomi, Barnabas discovered Paul in a cave, Julius Caesar teamed up with Brutus, Pippen dished to Jordan and Sonny sang perfectly with Cher. It's people discovering their *ezer kenegdos* and living a better life.

Just like Adam, we need to understand that we need community. We, too, need a team. We can't fulfill our purpose alone.

Person of Peace

In the Gospels, Jesus gave his disciples the updated version of the *ezer kenegdo*. As he sent out the 12 disciples in Luke 9, he encouraged them to look for the person of peace. He defined this person of peace as someone who meets the following three criteria. He or she is:

1. Interested in you and in what you have to say
2. Willing to serve you
3. Ready to open up their network to you

Jesus not only instructed them in this strategy, but lives it out as well. You see these three criteria met in his engagements with Peter, Nicodemus and the woman at the well, to name a few.

I've coached many leaders over the years who are frustrated with life. They assume the problems lie around what they are doing. The solutions seem difficult, but obvious: "I need to change jobs, or move departments, maybe sell the company or invest in something new." Often, however, it's a *who* issue, not a *what* issue. They are in the right job and doing the right things, but they're just alone or around toxic people. They're either sick of the pressure, being responsible for all the work or the negativity and cynicism surrounding them in the office.

Once these leaders realize the issue is people-related, we can work to change the right things, such as discovering like-minded individuals to partner with or healthier people to be around. When this happens spirits improve, productivity and optimism increase and things are happier at home. A higher quality of life is achieved while the tasks have largely stayed the same.

In this place of community, our desire is to become a family on mission—an extended family with a purpose. In this context we hold the power to change the world and change lives.

A Soldier's Mentality

There's a reason solitary confinement is so effective, and why it's used as a form of torture in prison and military situations. It's the same reason the devil tries to isolate us. We're the most vulnerable when we're alone. Our minds mess with us and lead us into temptations and tendencies that we would never fall for in the safe, healthy context of good friends and teammates. As the saying goes: "United we stand, divided we fall."

Here Paul's metaphor of the athlete and soldier, which we discussed earlier, can again be helpful. We need to approach this aspect of life (both personally and professionally) as soldiers, not athletes.

Many sports are individual, and even in team sports, the athlete thinks and trains largely on his or her own. The training is marked by personal discipline and self-leadership, often in a solo setting. Picture a Lolo Jones on early-morning training runs, Michael Phelps doing countless laps in the pool or Rory McIlroy playing endless rounds of golf.

Soldiers, on the other hand, never fight alone. It is always a communal activity. You wouldn't think to send one Navy SEAL off to fight a war. Being a soldier is always about banding together and fighting together *as one*. That's the whole point of boot camp—creating unity. The armies that win are the armies that fight together the best.

Paul understood this mindset, and in Ephesians 6 he spoke to the soldier in all of us, reminding us of the power of unity.

> Be strong in the Lord and in his mighty power. Put on all of God's armor so that you will be able to stand firm against all strategies of the devil. For we are not fighting against flesh-and-blood enemies, but against evil rulers and authorities of the unseen world, against mighty powers in this dark world, and against evil spirits in the heavenly places.
>
> Therefore, put on every piece of God's armor so you will be able to resist the enemy in the time of evil. Then after the battle you will still be standing firm. Stand your ground, putting on the belt of truth and the body armor of God's righteousness. For shoes, put on the peace that comes from the Good News so that you will be fully prepared. In addition to all of these, hold up the shield of faith to stop the fiery arrows of the devil. Put on salvation as your helmet, and take the sword of the Spirit, which is the word of God.
>
> Pray in the Spirit at all times and on every occasion. Stay alert and be persistent in your prayers for all believers everywhere. — Ephesians 6:10-18

Did you notice the one word Paul used multiple times in this chapter?

Stand. He says it three different times.

When you look at the original Greek for this passage, Paul writes *stand* in the plural.

"You guys" stand. "You guys" put on the reality of faith and truth of salvation and peace. It's not you—it's us. It's the body of Christ covered in the armor of God.

We *stand up* in relationship with God our Father, Jesus and the Holy Spirit. We *stand in* together as community, as we band together as one. Finally we *stand out*, as we seek to change the world, impacting others for the sake of his kingdom.

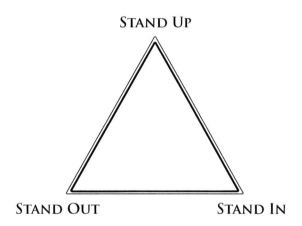

STAND UP

STAND OUT   STAND IN

Conclusion

Thankfully, Jesus perfectly displayed how to navigate this community balance. He understood the importance of depending on his Father and the Holy Spirit (up), while doing life with his disciples (in), in order to reach the world (out).

His leadership in community was powerful, which allowed him to change the course of history and still lead and influence people to this day. If we follow his lead, if our families, businesses and extended families follow his lead, we too will have access to the same power that will change the course of history and influence the lives of countless individuals.

If you're Batman, who's your Robin? As soldiers in a battle (which we all are), who are the mighty men and women surrounding you, as you also surround them?

Your team is vital. You need a team in order for your impossible dreams to become possible, and for your teammates' impossible dreams to become possible as well. *No one wins alone.*

A few years ago I went back and re-watched *The Rocketeer*. Sadly, it wasn't as good as I remembered it. Equally as sad, I realized how quickly my focus had gravitated toward the "hero" of the film. I completely missed the major team aspect of the movie. *The Rocketeer* didn't defeat the enemy on his own. Without the essential help of his good friend Mr. Peabody, Howard Hughes and his girlfriend, he would have lost. If only I'd picked up on that 24 years ago.

Discussion Questions

1. As you look at your life, do you tend toward individualism and isolation, or do you make concentrated efforts toward connection and community?

2. Are you too focused on the what rather than the who in your relationships?

3. Using the person of peace lens, do you see a potential team? Are there friends who could function as family? Personally? Professionally?

4. What repeatable patterns can you start in order to give access to your life to others, specifically with your family, co-workers and friends?

5. How can you communicate what you learned in this chapter to your family, friends and co-workers in order for them to come alongside you to help with the life changes you hope to apply?

Putting It Into Practice

Reuben Zuidhof: Co-founder, CEO of Adventure Teaching, Inc.

Little did I know that, when I brainstormed my first business with my college roommate in a South Korean coffee shop, it would set me on a life-changing trajectory. Our dream of a part-time business has now turned into three full-time businesses and a kingdom partnership. Our businesses exist to fuel a lifestyle that we are called to in Vancouver. Along with the support and strength of our wives, we have invited a few other families along for a journey that we call our *Vancouver Oikos*. Our *Vancouver Oikos* has really established itself through predictable patterns and directive leadership.

I figured that community would just happen here in Vancouver, Canada, and while it does, there is a point when it becomes complacent and stale. Yet, when we sent out calendar invites six months in advance for every Wednesday, we began to see consistency. We coupled that with directive leadership and an intentional pattern on Wednesdays, during which we rotate between invitational dinners, serving at a Ronald McDonald House and spending evenings together in prayer and worship. Through this intentionality God has opened our eyes to how community can make a profound impact on a city. True depth of relationships and loving each other speaks loudly in a city where loneliness often prevails. Only God knows where he'll take the *Vancouver Oikos*, but we're excited about the journey!

Chapter Seven
PRACTICALITIES: LIVING IT OUT

Great things are done by a series of small things brought together.
— Vincent Van Gogh

God works all things for good for those who love him.
— Romans 8:28

Leaders on a Different Level

I've been honored to know and connect with a lot of great leaders over the years. It's exciting to be around people who are smart, full of energy, passionate about their work and able to take teams and initiatives to the next level. However, every once in a while, I get to be around someone who's different—different in a way that takes greatness higher. I've only known a few of these individuals—men and women who have a presence about them, and who, when you interact with them, make you feel like the most important person in the room. These leaders are people of dynamic vision, character and charisma. They lead powerful causes and bring many people with them.

The first time I encountered this type of leader I was at Elanco, Eli Lilly's animal health division.

Jeff Simmons was a dynamic leader who cared about his employees, authentically engaged with customers, was passionate about the business and believed in the products. He was a leader at a whole other level.

He embodied the mission, vision and values of the company. All Five Capitals were in order for Jeff, and so he was willing to take the calculated risk, speak the unvarnished truth and make the moves to see the vision of "food enriching life" a reality each and every day. Best of all Jeff wasn't an obsessive workaholic; his personal life was in order as well. He enjoyed life, was fun to be around, had a great family and was involved in his church.

Where's Jeff Simmons now? He's still at Elanco, currently serving as president of this billion-dollar division of Lilly.

Being around great leaders like Jeff always causes me to wonder—does everyone have the potential to reach this level of passion, ability and fulfillment in life? Or is it just an elite few who have the open doors and opportunities, as well as the skills and abilities, to capture personal and professional success?

I think the door is wide open. After all, I know Jesus wasn't just talking to the elite when he made statements like:

"I have come to give you life and life to the full."[48]

"You can do everything I can do, and even greater things than these." [49]

Or even Paul's words: "I can do all things in Christ, who gives me strength."[50]

The better question isn't whether or not a full and fulfilling life is possible. It's *Where do I start?*

We start where Jesus ends. Toward the beginning of his ministry, he gave a State of the Union address (known as the Sermon on the Mount) in which he preached on the realities of how to live from a heavenly perspective. As we mentioned earlier, he chose to end this sermon with the parable of the wise and the foolish builders.

Simply put, the wise builder builds a life on two things: *humility* and *courage*.

He has the humility to hear and the courage to obey what he hears. (Here's why this is important: from an earthly perspective, not everything you hear will make sense. That's why courage is also required.)

What I've found is that most of us are really good at either one or the other, humility or courage. To be great at both hearing and doing requires time and effort. The great majority of committed Christians naturally gravitate toward either the hearing or the doing category. Let's take a closer look at the variations resident in most of the leaders we know and work with.

The Forgetful Person/Leader

These individuals are good at hearing from God and they enjoy that ability, whether it's from the Bible, books, sermons or nature. However, putting what they hear into practice can be a struggle. They are like the great seminary professor or an amazing basketball coach who knows what to do and even why to do it, but who isn't that great at implementation. In other words they can create the hype or expectation, but they aren't good at playing the game. They live by the (mostly unspoken) motto: "Do as I say, not as I do."

The Fumbling Person/Leader

These individuals are good at obedience, but not necessarily good at listening. So they stumble their way through life. They generally know the good they ought to do and the principles of the Bible, yet they don't create the space to specifically hear what God is saying to them. For example, if Joshua had said, "Yeah God, I got this battle—no worries" at Jericho, defeat would have come upon the Hebrew people. Instead, God had specific instructions as to how to defeat the enemy. Fumbling leaders are like the experienced Christians who generally know what to do, but can't disciple others. In basketball terms they are the star players who have lots of experience and instinct but lack the competency to explain it or teach it.

The Frustrated Person/Leader

These individuals go through life choosing to neither hear nor obey, and so they find plenty of frustration. Choosing to do life their own way, they find themselves out of the game—much like the player who rides the bench for the season unwilling to listen to the coach or work on the basic fundamentals of the game. This mentality will either bring an attitude of cynicism and negativity or a false arrogance, often with undertones of insecurity.

The Faithful Person/Leader

This, of course, is the wise builder—an individual who is slowly and steadily advancing by creating the space to humbly listen and courageously obey. Over the course of their life, two things become increasingly clear:

- ▶ Identity: who I am (values)
- ▶ Calling: what I'm called to do (vision)

This is similar to the Level 5 leaders described in Jim Collins' book, *Good to Great.* Their life and leadership draw people, as they are both compelling and contagious—attributes that produce a multipliable harvest (30-, 60-, or 100-fold) as well as the fruits of the Spirit. Their faithfulness builds into people, families, communities and organizations, as they bring life and love into this world.

Hearing and Doing / Humility and Courage

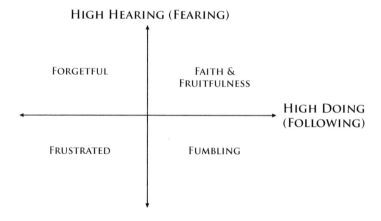

The First Step Toward a Better Life

A question I get regularly when speaking or coaching is this: "From a biblical perspective, what's the most important leadership trait?" Obviously there are a number of answers and opinions out there, and many of them could work. But what's number one? As we learned earlier from the parable of the wise builder, the most important leadership trait would definitely have to be *listening.*

Listening is tied to extraordinary lives and extraordinary leaders.

Becoming an extraordinary leader in the home, the workplace, at church and in your community starts with listening to God.

Jesus is the greatest leader and listener who ever lived. What he did with a core group of 12 people is

> ## LISTENING IS TIED TO EXTRAORDINARY LIVES AND EXTRAORDINARY LEADERS.

unbelievable, and he wants to lead us to this level. Here in John 10 he explains what that looks like:

> Jesus said, "Very truly I tell you Pharisees, anyone who does not enter the sheep pen by the gate, but climbs in by some other way, is a thief and a robber. The one who enters by the gate is the shepherd of the sheep. The gatekeeper opens the gate for him, and the sheep listen to his voice. He calls his own sheep by name and leads them out. When he has brought out all his own, he goes on ahead of them, and his sheep follow him because they know his voice. But they will never follow a stranger; in fact, they will run away from him because they do not recognize a stranger's voice."
> – John 10:1-5

If you're like me, you have big dreams to lead amazing organizations, lead phenomenal initiatives, lead your home and your spouse well and pursue the ideas and possibilities for your life.

If we want to reach life to the full, both as people and as leaders, listening to God is a value we need to take seriously.

Have you ever hung out with a couple that has been married for years and years? One starts a sentence and the other finishes it. Or maybe you have a friend with whom you banter back and forth, reciting one inside joke after another. This is the kind of intimacy we are after with God—a connection that is rich, deep and personal.

The reality is that most of us don't take the time to cultivate this relationship. But our relationship with our Father in heaven is just like any other relationship we have. It takes time to hear, to establish trust, to believe in his character and to know we can trust him.

When we take time to really listen, we'll know him. Slowly we'll learn to know him, not just in our head, but with our heart as well. Witnessing that he is faithful, powerful, present everywhere and wise, we will experience his love for us and how he speaks to us. This process allows us to trust him as we grow in greater fear and humility and, of course, courage.

If you want to increase your influence and impact, then spend time discerning how the Father speaks to you. Don't worry if this takes time and effort. In Christ, there is no condemnation. It's not about whether you have been perfect; it's about taking the time to cultivate the relationship.

Whatever your aspirations are—if you want to be the mom, the spouse, the business leader, the entrepreneur, the CEO—then get serious about listening and growing in confidence at discerning his voice. In and through you, he'll do great things and you'll influence many. May we be emboldened, convicted and encouraged to grow in confidence and competency at hearing his voice, so we can find his way and walk in it.

My Listening Story

Three years ago I was leading a business leaders workshop in Cincinnati for approximately 30 people. Toward the end there was an opportunity to share information on some coaching and consulting opportunities we could offer to those who were interested. Surveying the crowd, I could tell by their faces who was interested and who was not interested.

After I finished talking, God prompted me to connect with a husband and a wife sitting toward the back. This couple hadn't given any visual indication they were connecting with the material I was presenting. However, working to trust God's leading, I made a point to thank them for coming. To my surprise, the husband, Chris, said he had enjoyed the material, but did have a few questions and concerns, which we were able to talk through. Fast forward three years and Chris and I are great friends. I've been coaching him and his team for the past two and a half years.

Chris has what I consider a really cool business—his company makes all the lining for every American-made football in the world. Chris also has a passion for family, and his eight kids are tangible proof of that. This passion has turned into a ministry called The New Frontier, which enables dads and sons to go on adventure weeks in Montana and use this time to help them understand who they are in Christ and the adventure to which God calls them. Thanks to God's prompting and some investment, my wife and I love having the privilege to serve alongside Chris and his wife, Ruthie, as they seek to help others connect to the perspective and priorities of their Father in heaven. This relationship all grew from my decision to disregard logic and obey God's voice.

The best part of it all? It doesn't matter where you are—whether you're flying high through life or at the bottom of a pit, God will meet you right there and take both your personal and professional life to another level. Sure, there might be difficult choices, or a change in priorities or investments, but the price will be worth the prize. Recalibrate your perspectives, rethink your potential, realign your priorities, review your practices and choose to humbly hear and courageously obey. Then see what Jesus the builder can do.

He wants to build your life.

He wants to help you build a better life.

Discussion Questions

1. Reflect on your life. Do you know any compelling and contagious leaders like my former boss, Jeff? What sets them apart? What character traits would you like to imitate?

2. Humbly hearing builds your character. Courageously obeying builds your competency. Which one do you need to focus on?

3. Did you relate most to the forgetful leader, the fumbling leader or the frustrated leader? Based on where you are on this matrix, what needs to change in your life?

4. How can you take a step toward being a more faithful person and leader?

5. Where are you today? How are you asking God to help you build a better life? Are there any specific areas that you want him to break through?

Putting It Into Practice

Eric Vogel, Enterprise Architect and Systems Engineer at TeraLogics, LLC

It's been a ton of fun the past few years witnessing God bring so many breakthroughs into my life and the lives of those within the Five Capitals family. More than three years ago, I realized my deep desire to live an integrated life— to have my marriage, family, friends, church, ministry and work life all pointing in the same direction. I was encouraged to put first things first by reordering my priorities, starting with my time spent abiding with Jesus and my most significant relationships. I quickly realized that an integrated life starts first with my relationship with the Father and second a relationship with my wife, Katie, built on a common vision and values. I was empowered to have intentional conversations with Katie, which often weren't easy, but they were necessary.

Now, three years later, Katie and I are both making consistent time to rest and abide, plus we now have friends who are family (framily!) and family who are friends. Often, on my way to work, Katie and I talk on the phone about what we're excited and hopeful for God to do and what he is saying, and then we pray about how we plan to respond to him. Katie and I feel like we're on the same page with God and each other. We're now a family on mission! I'm so grateful to the Five Capitals team and the level of intentionality and breakthrough they've brought about in my life.

As it relates to work, the experience of a demotion due to contractual downsizing two years ago crushed my identity as I battled with my desire for approval, promotion and corporate success. Simply confessing and talking through my disappointment with my coach and others on the call was hard, but necessary. It gave me the inner strength and freedom to face my exterior battles and talk about them with my wife and even my friends. In the midst of these conversations, my coach and huddle group were there to give hope, stress-relieving insight and freeing perspectives.

Prior to this circumstance, our coach had prepared us well to respond (not react) to events such as these and had encouraged me to imagine where my professional relationships could be in five, 10 and 20 years. Rather than harboring resentment, I received a peace about my current position and career knowing that it is God—not my boss—who fights my battles and tells me who and whose I am. My idea of success was redeemed. I'm confident that this battle was necessary for me to understand my God-given identity. By God's grace I made it through with a thankful heart and will use this experience to empower those who struggle with their purpose.

Now, two years later, I still have peace about my career, knowing it doesn't define me. I'm a better husband, co-worker, friend and family member—more fun to work with, less stressed and empowered with greater clarity. My prayer is to steadily grow to become a spiritual giant, inspiring those around me to bolster their faith, family and relationships amidst the demands of a career.

PRESSING FORWARD: EXPERIENCING LASTING CHANGE

There was a season of my life when I loved going to conferences. Business conferences, marketing conventions, workshops, seminars—you name it, I was there. The buzz, the people, inspiring speakers, new product designs and ideas and plenty of inspiration to go around had me excited. And I got to experience all this on the company's time and dime! Best of all, it didn't feel like work, as I got to see a new city, eat at fun restaurants and meet great people.

Cleaning out my desk drawer one day, I came across a number of the conference packets I had collected over the years. Quickly flipping through some of them, I realized that attending most of these events was a waste. While I am sure some nuggets of information seeped into my subconscious, little of my daily perspective and routine had changed.

Too often we read the book, attend the conference or watch the TED Talk, only to go back to normal. Without coaches and guides, community and accountability, few inspirational messages actually result in change.

Therefore, I extend to you one final challenge. If you've found any of the concepts or frameworks helpful, encouraging or even inspiring, take this opportunity to make some changes to build a better life. Ask friends to hold you accountable, seek out a mentor or find a coach to help ensure these potentially life-changing concepts don't get placed on a shelf or in a drawer.

One of our company values is this: *Life Transformation over Clever Information.* Yes, learning new concepts and clever insights is fun and engaging. Our commitment, however, is to ensure you're actually living into the changes you'd like to see in your life by overcoming barriers and capturing opportunities.

This is why we always challenge people who engage with us to find that coach and community who will help get them to the next level. If these people don't exist, talk to us about Five Capitals coaching. Developing others is our primary focus. We have a fantastic team—each member with a unique skill set and specialty. We're able to meet you where you are, discern a path forward and keep you going. We know it takes both inspiration as well as perspiration to change. We're willing to go through this with you.

To learn more about Five Capitals coaching, consulting and our workshops, visit us at fivecapitals.net or email us at jo@fivecapitals.net

We look forward to journeying with you.

Don't just take our word for it. See what others have to say about coaching with Five Capitals.

Krissy Little
— Marketing Department, Procter & Gamble / Independent Consultant

My coaching calls have been a wonderful investment that I would recommend to anyone who wants to see personal and professional growth. I have seen significant positive changes in my life in just the three short months I have worked with my coach. I started the coaching calls to get greater clarity on the purpose of my business. Where I previously felt confused and frustrated, I now feel joy, peace and focus. Although my business was my primary reason for the coaching, I have also seen tremendous progress in my spiritual and relational (family/marriage) health. Every week I'm receiving new tools and homework that enable me to take new ground in all areas of my life. My husband and I are now meeting with a Five Capitals coach, and I'm so excited about how God will use the coaching calls to help us strengthen our marriage.

Chuck Proudfit
— Founder/CEO, At Work On Purpose

My Five Capitals coaching experience has had a significant impact on my life. My coach's skill in presenting concepts clearly and simply has made it easier for me to apply discipleship tools to my work and home environments. In particular, his teaching has enabled me to hone in on "people of peace" that I need on my team at work, and he has fostered accountability for me to work from rest. He is well versed biblically and shines when connecting Scripture to teaching concepts.

Through the coaching and consulting I've received, my leadership skills and abilities have dramatically improved. Others have noticed my ability to connect biblical concepts—like Oikos (or missional community)—to creative applications in my own work environment. I've been experiencing major breakthrough in the areas of content documentation, strategic pilot testing and creating reproducible systems—all thanks to the benefit of interactive dialogue with my coach. Additionally, my coach is one of the finest active listeners I have ever met. He is exceptional at understanding what others share and then repackaging it in a concise and precise summary.

Last but not least, all the Five Capitals team members (with whom I've interacted) have significant leadership gifts—both in thought and action. They share a rare capacity to synthesize information into penetrating insight, coupled with consistent follow-through, strong interpersonal skills and adaptive teamwork. The leaders who enter into a coaching/consulting relationship will know that they are in relationship with skilled practitioners.

Dora and Steve Manuel
— Owners, Viva Bella Event Planning & High Five Salon

Through our time in working with our Five Capitals coach, our family's rhythms have changed dramatically for the better. Our coach has helped us process and apply great biblical teaching around the way our home works, as well as helped to shepherd us through significant changes in both of our businesses. We are running them more confidently and biblically, which is awesome.

Additionally, as a CoCEO married couple, we have a greater sense of vision and (because of that) know what our next steps are, moving forward. Our coach's leadership has helped in several arenas: from basing our schedules on the Five Capitals framework to giving MyersBriggs training to both of our corporate staffs, to calling us to accountability for what God is saying to us on a weekly basis. I would strongly encourage anyone to get some regular time with a Five Capitals coach—but you can't have ours!

Melissa Rogers
— Medical ER Doctor and Department Head, St. Joseph Hospital System

I have been in a Five Capitals coaching huddle for about five months, and perhaps the most significant result has been learning to live a fully integrated life. As is often the case, I can be one person at work and a totally different person at home, in the community or at church. I have never been able to bridge the two successfully. This year has been a journey of getting to the root causes of that inconsistency. Much of the disconnect has been rooted in not understanding my true identity as a child of God. My Five Capitals coach has done a great job presenting the issues/questions at the root of this and then holding us in that place until we hear the voice of God as it relates to our identity and calling. I can't believe how much life change I've seen in the past year. My coach is famous in my home (and now in my current huddles) for asking, "What is the one next step that you can take today to live into what you believe God is calling you to?" Transformation is a process of taking one step at a time.

Though I am not a shapes person, I have found the concepts contained within the shapes to be a very, very helpful approach in terms of simplifying things we are tempted to make way too difficult. It has been so freeing to learn biblical concepts that can so obviously and readily be applied both at home and at work. Probably the biggest breakthrough in regard to that is understanding that because we are children of God, we carry the authority of God and therefore can exercise the power of God—everywhere, all the time! How cool is that! I grew up in a tradition that never spoke of the power of God to heal, to restore and to transform. That realization has totally changed the direction of my life, my family and my work.

To close, we were laughing in our coaching huddle last week because, while we have been meeting on the phone for months, we have never met each other face to face. And yet all of us are growing and being transformed. As business professionals we are family on this call, offering love, support, encouragement and accountability to each other. It is my testimony that with a skilled coach, God can work through any issues/questions and conversations even though we are miles apart.

Peter Zimmer

— Owner, Huff Realty, a Berkshire Hathaway Affiliate

One of the biggest areas of change our coaching calls have made in our lives is around family rhythms. I'm a business owner with a crazy schedule, and as much as I've tried, my family has always seemed to get what was left over from me. Our coach has amazingly helped us establish regular rhythms of rest and work, putting "rocks in the river" to promote health in my family and capacity in my business. Now I am more in control of my business and excited when it's growing, rather than allowing it to control me so I'm stressing out and cheating my family. I feel like I have my life back.

Scot Sustad

— CEO, Digital Hot Sauce Inc.

Life as an entrepreneur and small business owner can be very isolating. The endless drive toward growth and keeping up with the current pace of life in the business world is intoxicating and exhausting. It isn't unusual to look back and see that a surprising span of time that has gone by without genuine and lasting relational connection. With Five Capitals coaching, I've continually sought to pan back, prioritize and further develop significant and personal relationships that impact and enrich my entire life, both at work and home.

Chris Hartenstein

— CEO, Hartco Corporation

There are many ways in which the huddle time with my Five Capitals coach has been beneficial. First, he has challenged my thinking as I've processed the things God's been saying to me about my leadership as it relates to my business. He's helped me filter out my own assumptions and preconceived ideas to be a better listener to God's voice. As God's desires have become clearer, my coach has then helped me process the most appropriate next steps using Christ as the model. We have also had some very real and difficult discussions about my family's relationships, rhythms, habits and struggles. Each of these times has led to significant changes at home and to leading me to a more integrated life.

Speaking of the home front, there have been significant changes in the rhythms in my life. There were certainly areas of my life where I had fallen into a rut as opposed to being in a groove. Slowing down and learning how to abide has been very significant. As a driving leader, I never saw how always being busy and pushing actually made me more tired and less effective than living a balanced life of rest and work does. I actually accomplish more now, with better results and less stress than I ever have had in my career.

Other helpful aspects have been the discussions surrounding how Jesus led well, especially in the areas of mission, purpose, team development, casting vision, training others, impactful teaching and releasing leaders. I love seeing Jesus as my primary model. Like my coach always says, "No matter the topic, Jesus is always the smartest guy in the room."

It's cool how both my wife and colleagues have noticed how I stop, pray and process more versus trying to solve problems on my own strength. Although I have always been a participative manager, now I am actually discipling the guys in their leadership, not just correcting their behavior. This has allowed for more meaningful conversations and has enabled me to pull back the curtain to share how to make a decision. It has also helped them see my heart in leading as I slow down to help communicate and genuinely invest in their lives.

Lastly, thanks to my coach, my biggest breakthrough is in how I see myself within my business. Before the coaching started, in my heart and mind my role within the corporation was in doubt. I was bored, disinterested and frustrated. Through various conversations, prayer, Bible reading and discussion on how Jesus led, it became very clear what the Lord's will was for me within the company. It has been very freeing and has allowed me to see how others can become a greater part of our company, with greater responsibility and opportunities to grow— allowing me to pursue many new and exciting areas of calling.

Matt & Betsy Wilhelm
— American Heart Association, Regional Manager / Stay-at-Home Mom
From Matt:

Just under a year ago, I found myself wondering why my relationship with the Lord was so stagnant. I was stuck in a place of thinking that just believing was good enough. When my wife and I entered into a coaching relationship with Five Capitals, I became aware of the invitation God had given me to know him more intimately. Our coach challenged me with establishing a daily rhythm of conversation with God. As I spent each morning with him, I began to realize that he was speaking to me. Our coach has taken God's words for me and helped me to understand what to do with them—how to create a plan around it and ask for accountability with carrying it out. My relationship with God has truly grown more in the past seven months than in the previous 35 years. It's a relationship that continues to grow more each day—and what's so cool is that God is speaking to me about my work life as well, giving me tools and strategies through the coaching to really make a difference for Christ each and every day.

From Betsy:
As we reflect on the past seven months of coaching calls, we have seen incredible life changes in us, our marriage, family and community. There are, however, some common themes that spread across our transformation that we would like to highlight.

Individual Transformation: When I think back to who I was seven months ago, I cannot say enough about the life and light that has touched me since we have started our coaching calls. In this time, I have learned that my heavenly Dad approves of me and loves me. There is nothing I can do to earn this priceless gift, and I am worthy because he made me. My identity has been cemented in this understanding and it has radically changed my life.

My relationships with my husband, children, family and friends are richer and deeper because I rest in the knowledge that my Father loves me. I thirst for the Lord, and our relationship has left a sweet and intimate imprint on my life. I am confident in the still, small voice that I hear, and I am learning to trust and understand who he is and I willingly want my life to reflect him. I am amazed how God has used my coach in so many real and specific ways. The calls have led me to understand the sweet and powerful character of God, and I can't help but dream about what God will do with my life in the years to come.

Marriage: The tools and wisdom shared with us on the calls have created a significant and intimate change in our marriage. We are now equipped to understand the individual and marvelous ways that God has created each of us. We are very uniquely and distinctly designed, but we have learned to appreciate our differences and are now operating as a marriage that complements and supports each other. We have become intentional in putting each other first, and a love has blossomed that is beyond desiring a good or even great marriage. Together, we are an intricately woven pattern that God uses to teach us, love us and lead our family and community. A phrase that our coach has taught us sums up the commitment we have completely invested in each other and our marriage: We are each other's "Forever and Every Day Friend".

Family: As these calls have led us in our individual and marriage journeys, it has impacted our family in deep and lasting ways. While there are many components of this coaching that we could highlight, the two biggest factors are: 1) helping us uncover the vision and values God has instilled in us for our family. We are beyond excited to take this journey and to live out the passion and purpose that God has planted in our hearts. It was a hard and sometimes frustrating journey, but our coach helped us to navigate our course and always encouraged us back to the Word and God's purpose for our life. 2) We also have found such freedom in understanding and believing in rhythms (daily, weekly, monthly and yearly) and working from rest. We are establishing intentional rhythms with our children, family and community. Our life is beginning to flourish out of abiding in the Lord, and we have been freed from the burden of striving or the fear of not being equipped to disciple our children.

Danita Bye
— Founder & CEO, Dakota Leadership
The top three reasons I work with Brandon and Five Capitals:

1. Being a leader can be lonely. Being a leader committed to following Jesus can be even lonelier—it's difficult to find people to collaborate with who get the importance of being a good steward in all of life, including home, work and community. Brandon lives the reality of whole-life discipleship and encourages others on their journey.

2. In the past, I've often felt that my involvement with business wasn't really kingdom work and that the Bible didn't speak to my business problems. Brandon continually challenges and encourages me with the everyday applicability of Scripture so I operate in a wiser way at home, at work and in the community.

3. I'm a conceptual thinker; therefore I need someone who can help me incorporate big ideas into practical steps. The Five Capitals tools help in that process.

ABOUT THE AUTHOR
BRANDON SCHAEFER

Brandon is the Executive Director of Five Capitals. Five Capitals works with Business Leaders offering Coaching and Consulting to help them to change their lives and grow their business. The focus is to help them live an integrated life, discover life to the full and increase their spiritual/strategic confidence in the workplace. Five Capitals works with all types of people and organizations equipping them to reach their full potential. Brandon has coached hundreds of individuals, groups and couples over the years. A sought-after speaker all over the world, he has engaged with thousands through workshops and conferences, as business / church leaders seek to benefit from the Five Capital principles.

Brandon is a graduate of Iowa State University with majors in international business, agricultural business and Spanish. After graduating, he worked for Motorola in Glasgow, Scotland, and for Eli Lilly and Company in Indianapolis, both in their strategic marketing departments.

After years in the corporate world, Brandon was called to work in the local church. Since then he has completed a master's degree in leadership from Indiana Wesleyan University and a master's degree in biblical studies from Asbury Seminary. In ministry, Brandon served as the adult discipleship pastor at East 91st Street Christian Church in Indianapolis, and most recently as the pastor of discipleship, leadership and outreach ministries at Southland Christian Church in Lexington, Kentucky. He currently lives in Pawleys Island, South Carolina, with his lovely wife, T.J. They have two daughters, Eva and Teagan.

ABOUT FIVE CAPITALS: GLOBAL INITIATIVES

We help people and organizations go after all God has for them in life. Five Capitals is a global initiative working with business and church leaders in the areas of personal development, leadership skills and organizational growth strategies. Using an integrated approach, we help leaders see how the Bible connects to both their home and work, creating greater levels of wholeness, influence and fulfillment.

Our team has a passion for engaging people and teams to see greater levels of health, productivity and profitability. We invest transformational tools and skills, allowing for a more fulfilling, impactful and productive life. These tools are simple, memorable and reproducible, creating a common language and allowing participants to pass them on to others.

We equip leaders to:
- ▶ Integrate Their Life
- ▶ Increase Their Impact
- ▶ Discover Life to the Full

Visit our website to learn more about:
- ▶ Coaching and Consulting Options
- ▶ Equipping Workshops and Seminars
- ▶ Global Partnership Initiatives
- ▶ Sermon Series Curriculum
- ▶ Becoming a Five Capitals Coach

Connect with us at: jo@fivecapitals.net | 843.461.5935

FIVECAPITALS.NET

ENDNOTES

---

[1] http://www.brainyquote.com/citation/quotes/quotes/d/davidallan204305.html?ct=David+Allan+Coe

[2] *Renovation of the Heart* by Dallas Willard, page 241

[3] Luke 4:28-30

[4] http://www.greatsite.com/timeline-english-bible-history/john-wycliffe.html

[5] Matthew 16:18

[6] Matthew 7:24-27

[7] John 10:10

[8] I first heard this teaching on his word, his works, and his ways by Mike Breen and Dave Rhodes. It has proved crucial to my perspective on how Jesus builds my life and those around me.

[9] John 1:40-42

[10] Matthew 16:23

[11] I am indebted to Andy Stanley for this way of putting it.

[12] http://appleinsider.com/articles/12/01/13/former_apple_ceo_john_sculley_says_he_never_fired_co_founder_steve_jobs

[13] I first heard of this matrix from Mike Breen and it is also highlighted in his book *Covenant and Kingdom*. Dave Rhodes helped me to create the development and delivery matrix, especially in thinking through how to unpack it in everyday life.

14   http://www.eyewitnesstohistory.com/landrush.htm

15   See Philippians 3:14

16   See Ephesians 6:12

17   See John 17:21

18   https://hbr.org/2005/11/are-you-working-too-hard

19   Matthew 17:5

20   See Philippians 4:13

21   From a journal entry dated October 28, 1949. Quoted in *The Shadow of the Almighty*, by Elisabeth Elliot.

22   http://newsfeed.time.com/2012/11/28/500-million-powerball-jackpot-the-tragic-stories-of-the-lotterys-unluckiest-winners/slide/william-post/

23   See Matthew 6:19-34 for the whole context.

24   http://www.thefreedictionary.com/capital

25   Matthew 25:23

26   Case in point: the rich young ruler we discussed earlier.

27   John 14:12

28   Luke 8:2-3

29   Mark 6:31

30   John 15:1-8

31   Exodus 20:8-11

32   Ephesians 5:15-17

33   Matthew 7:28-29

34   Matthew 22:15-22

35 Matthew 22:23-33

36 One such study from 2010 can be found at http://content.time.com/time/magazine/article/0,9171,2019628,00.html.

37 Acts 20:35

38 For more on the study, see Norton's TED Talk entitled "How to Buy Happiness," http://www.ted.com/talks/michael_norton_how_to_buy_happiness.html

39 We have developed a tool called the Learning Circle that helps people answer these questions. You can read about it in our book *Building a Discipling Culture*.

40 John 3:16

41 Matthew 22:37-40

42 I have a video blog post available at fivecapitals.net that delves more deeply into Myers-Briggs and the Five Capitals.

43 They're listed in 2 Samuel 23.

44 John 5:19

45 John 10:30

46 John 17:21

47 Genesis 2:18

48 John 10:10

49 John 14:12

50 Philippians 4:13